GUNS + TACOS

Season One, Volume 2
Subscriber Edition

GUNS + TACOS

Season One
Tacos de Cazuela con Smith & Wesson by Gary Phillips
Three Brisket Tacos and a Sig Sauer by Michael Bracken
A Gyro and a Glock by Frank Zafiro
Three Chalupas, Rice, Soda...and a Kimber .45 by Trey R. Barker
Some Churros and El Burro by William Dylan Powell
A Beretta, Burritos, and Bears by James A. Hearn

Trey R. Barker, William Dylan Powell and James A. Hearn

GUNS + TACOS

Season One, Volume 2
Subscriber Edition

SERIES CREATED AND EDITED BY
MICHAEL BRACKEN & TREY R. BARKER

Down & Out Books
3959 Van Dyke Road, Suite 265
Lutz, FL 33558
DownAndOutBooks.com

The characters and events in this book are fictitious. Any similarity to real persons,
living or dead, is coincidental and not intended by the author.

Cover design by Zach McCain

ISBN: 1-64396-126-8
ISBN-13: 978-1-64396-126-2

CONTENTS

Three Chalupas, Rice, Soda…and a Kimber .45   1
Trey R. Barker

Some Churros and El Burro   61
William Dylan Powell

A Beretta, Burritos, and Bears   117
James A. Hearn

Platanos con Lechera and a Snub-Nosed .38   167
Michael Bracken

There's a taco truck in Chicago known among a certain segment of the population for its daily specials. Late at night and during the wee hours of the morning, it isn't the food selection that attracts customers, it's the illegal weapons available with the special order. Each episode of *Guns + Tacos* features the story of one Chicagoland resident who visits the taco truck seeking a solution to life's problems, a solution that always comes in a to-go bag.

GUNS + TACOS · CREATED AND EDITED BY  MICHAEL BRACKEN & TREY R. BARKER

TREY R. BARKER

THREE CHALUPAS, RICE, SODA AND A KIMBER .45

SEASON 1

EPISODE 4

BOOKS BY TREY R. BARKER

The Jace Salome Novels
Slow Bleed
East of the Sun
When the Lonesome Dog Barks

The Barefield Trilogy
2,000 Miles to Open Road
Exit Blood
Death is Not Forever

Stand-Alone Novels
No Harder Prison
The Unknowing

THREE CHALUPAS, RICE, SODA...AND A KIMBER .45

Trey R. Barker

Now—Sunday, 2:17 a.m.

Three blocks away and the lights are like cigarettes burning through a black blanket. Some people are visible in the fog of those lights. Grabbing food, sucking booze from brown paper bags. Eyes up and down, looking for whatever night people looked for at two in the damned morning.

Getting a taco, silly, Shannon asks, her voice forever twelve years old in your head. *It's a taco truck.*

Bullshit. You been a copper now almost sixteen years and you know what this truck is all about.

"Gotta smoke?" a voice asks.

You spin, right foot back, fists up and ready to War. Get the first punch—hit his gun hand, fuck up his shot—maybe snatch his gun, put it against his head.

Pull his own trigger. Snuff out his light.

Except...not his face. A different face. A homeless guy, reeking of shit booze and shittier drugs. Dressed in Goodwill specials, two different shoes on mismatched socks.

"Lookit you," the guy says. "All het-up to do some killing." The man screeches a sound like a screaming raccoon going under the wheels of a car.

"No," you say, heart slowing, breath cooling. *Not here to kill me...not to kill me.*

The man croaks a bloody laugh. "What the fuck ever, boy."

The two of you surrounded by buildings; wet brick, dirty, scabrous. Air full of the funk of blood and piss; the perfume of shit. You're comfortable in this smell, worked the streets your entire career. Comfort, maybe even relief?

Home with the stank, you think.

"Can see it in your eyes, boy." The homeless man shakes his head. "That's your thing, I ain't down for no killing."

Killed like Shannon?

Bloody and forgotten and lying in a ditch for the critters to eat and shit out?

It's not the fall that'll kill you. You've fallen before and you popped the landing. No, it's not the fall, it's the landing; pop feet first and you survive. Smash headfirst into the concrete?

"Yeah," you say. "There's some killing left to do."

Then—Last Sunday, 2:17 p.m.

Seriously? Were people just fucking stupid?

You hadn't needed any of the special training—six classes, forty hours each, exams and practicals—to handle this ad. It was all right out in the open.

Come see Daddy, Daughter, and do exactly as he says. He will tie you up and you will answer his every command.

This excited you. Not *what* they were looking for, that made you want to vomit and don a cape and blue tights and leap from tall buildings in a single bound while saving the world—*saving Shannon...saving all the Shannons*—but *that* they were looking. Their search was what excited you. Because in their searching, you found them and would catch them and quiet your own demons for a while.

"Then let's get it," you said, cranking up your undercover personality; a thirteen-year-old girl named Shannon. Named for your lost Shannon.

Which picture should you send?

The coy pictures of her on the beach with her family (in a swimsuit)? Or holding hands with a friend while roller skating (pic taken from behind)? Or petting a small dog (bending over and the barest hint of breast buds exposed)? Or...or...or...So many pics to choose from.

She's a pretty girl, Shannon said.

"Woman. She's twenty-six years old."

Still looks sixteen, Shannon said.

'She' is another officer, Ashlee, from your suburban Chicago department. She told you with a glint in her eye that she had no problem with you using her pictures to catch these guys. She was the first to call you *Perv Master*.

"Nasty fuckers," she had said. "Getting their ya-yas off on little girls." She had eyed you, deconstructed your soul. "You?

Like the deputy in McHenry County? Ten counts...predatory sex."

It was always the question beneath the surface, a variation on "how can you look at this stuff?" No one had ever asked it as brutally as she had over BLTs and brews. So, you manned up, faced her, and held her eyes tight as steel mesh. "There is nothing sexually exciting about a young girl. Or a young boy. Or watching a grown-up molest them. It's not funny or natural or an illustration of love or whatever those guys' rationalization is. It's rape. Period. The deputy in McHenry County ought to be shot. Period."

She had smiled, a tourmaline fire burning in her eyes. "Good answer."

After lunch, she had given you eleven pix and her digits and you had used both ever since.

You read the new ad again. *Come see Daddy...do...as he says...answer his every command.*

"Daddy Commander," you said.

Emailed him through the service, called Flip, that posted the ad. Hidden email addresses and ad reference numbers, all designed to keep people away from each other until they were ready to come together and do their thing.

You thought for a minute and typed: *Dear Daddy Commander, I'm too naughty for you to tie up.*

Attached a picture, nothing sexy, nothing revealing: Shannon walking to school.

SEND and gone.

"Another one, Shannon."

Good boy, she said.

Now—Sunday, 2:21 a.m.

Nerves are on fire. Fucking cliché. Twitching and sparking, beautiful purple and blue arcs. Electricity at the end of a downed power line. Remember the AC/DC album cover, the guitar guy all blasted up with electricity.

Makes you feel powerful, ready to War.

You wish he was here right now. Right this second. Hell yeah. Step into the street, lay the bullets down, see who comes out at the end.

Harsh truth? No idea where the cocksucker is. He's texted, threats and promises, but hasn't faced up yet. But you know it's coming tonight. We're done playing. Time to yank a trigger and finish this.

A handful of people are still at the taco truck, their faces ashen in the high-pressure sodium streetlamps. The orange light hollows out their faces, shadows their eyes, zombies the skin on their skulls. Some going home, some just coming out, some waiting to see what else the night still holds.

Chick looks at you, mouth wrapped around a burrito that bleeds red sauce. Sneering, looks you up and down, chews, swallows. "Twenty bucks for your burrito."

"Taquito," you say. "Wouldn't be worth your time."

Stumbles away in high heels, disappears into the darkness.

A woman behind the counter in the truck laughs.

"*Muchas grandes* burrito." He mimics a giant swinging dick. "Dress or no."

A guy, wearing a wife-beater and black bandanna around his forehead, sporting a teardrop tattoo below his right eye, laughs. "Wha'choo want, *jefe*?"

"Jessie."

The man squints, as though he can see you better through partially closed eyes. "Got no Jessie."

"No Jesse," the woman says.

You look pointedly at a third man, a hulk sitting in the corner, eyes closed.

The counterman waves him away. "Muerte."

"Breathes pretty good for a dead man," you say.

The man opens a single eye, focuses on you. "So do you." But he ignores you the way 'bangers do when they want you to think they don't consider you a threat.

You pull a wad of cash, and say, "Jessie. Or Jesse. I don't care which."

The dead man has both eyes open and on you now. Pretends a man in handcuffs. "*La pasma.*"

Jesse stares, his gaze gone from amused to angry. His hands clench and his jaw tightens. "Get the fuck out, *puta.*"

Jesse pulls a knife from under the counter. There is no glint under the lights. The finish is dull and stained, but you are certain the blade is as sharp as needed.

Muerte grunts a sound at them and they glance at him. When he nods, they step away from the counter.

You step up, crowding them with your full height, eyes hard, but hands out palms up. Calm. Unthreatening. "No *pasma.* No badge tonight." You push the money across the counter. "I want Jessie. Or Jesse. I want the daily special. Now. Or we *are* going to have a fucking problem."

Then—Last Sunday, 6:31 p.m.

"Sergeant." The voice boomed.

Lieutenant Terry McCann glared at you, his phony smile pasted like first grade artwork on his doughy face. He was a rumpy little fuck; a former Marine who loved to boast about how thoroughly he had stomped The Crucible during his boot camp time.

"Wonder how that worked," another former Marine, now detective, liked to quip. "Boot camp in 1985…Crucible started in 1996."

"Time travel," another officer, this guy from the Navy, always said. "He's a time-traveling Jarhead."

Other Marines-cum-cops told you The Crucible was something like fifty hours, fifty miles, seventy pounds of gear, rifle, two meals, maybe six hours of sleep. Then up a mountain and those who didn't die got their globe and anchor insignia and officially became Marines. You couldn't imagine McCann actually putting on a pack and hiking across the fucking parking lot, much less banging the entire Crucible.

"Sir," you said, trying to spin up something akin to respect.

"You get the memo about radio problems, Sergeant?"

"Straight up, Terry." His face twisted just a touch, he hated the personalization so you, of course, tweaked him when you could. "My guys come to me, I keep a list of dates and times and locations, give 'em to you. Through channels on any problems my guys' portable radios present while completing their assigned tasks, per your previous memo about chain of command."

Sucked his teeth and tried to figure out if your tone and word choice was meant to fuck with him.

News Flash: it was.

Secondary News Flash: he wouldn't figure it.

Tertiary New Flash: same old song and dance.

Eventually, confused in his own head about you and where your loyalties could be found—Quaternary News Flash: sort of to the department, but mostly to a dead girl you knew in junior high school before a man snatched her off the street, raped her, killed her, left her body, and walked away because none of it could be proven.

McCann nodded stiff and formal. Then a shoulder touched the wall and he slumped the slightest bit, almost imperceptibly. For a split second, he was the man who'd been your shift partner and from whom you'd learned the streets. Grapevine had him slowly strangling beneath the financial grip of three ex-wives, bad stock market and day trading choices, and on-going diabetic issues. For that moment, that son of a bitch was human again and you felt for him and wondered how he was digging his way out from under the pile.

Grapevine says he isn't.

But then he was Lieutenant. McCann again, jabbing his finger in your chest about some paperwork you'd missed and fuck that motherfucker. You wanted to spit on his boots or give him your Mama's stink eye. Instead, you were the model of a professionalism he didn't deserve.

"Make damn sure you get that shit done, Sergeant. No more foul ups."

"Hey, man. Come on. You okay?" you asked.

He opened his mouth, closed it again. "Yeah, just..." He took a deep, exhausted breath. Rubbed his forefinger and thumb together. "Notta gotta lotta. Anyway. Listen, Perv Master, just a heads up. Gilliam gets out next month."

"*Sergeant* Perv Master." Your nickname didn't sound great in his mouth; he's not one of the guys anymore. *Quit trying, Lt. Phony Baloney.* "On the seventeenth. Wanted more years but..." You shrugged. Guy got twelve years for possession and distribution of child pornography; not a great pounding but decent.

And Shannon got life so how good a pounding was it really?

McCann said, "Wouldn't'a gotten that many if you hadn't

worked your ass off. You did good."

"Well, thanks, but nothing helps a thin case grow fat like his buddies sending him more kiddie porn three days before I knock on his damned door."

McCann nodded. "Shitty timing for him, I guess."

"Happens that way. When I worked that Federal task force we had a guy doing automatic downloads while he was gone, remember? We kick the door, he's at work, but his giant screen TV is showing all the shit that was downloading while he was gone. Email dumps happen all the time, probably more often than we realize."

"Probably." Without another word, he penguined into the watch commander's office. Through the glass you saw him sit on the edge of the desk for a second, then slip heavily into the chair, the weight of years on him, then grab the phone and smash his fingers into the dial pad.

Back in your office two minutes later, you glanced at your computer.

Twenty-seven minutes.

That's how long it took this new guy to get back to you. Twenty-seven minutes wasn't the fastest response ever but it wasn't bad. Not a single email, either. While you were talking to McCann, Daddy Commander had sent fourteen emails.

Back when command first assigned you this gig, you didn't even know about the ads. A colleague at Chicago PD turned you on to them and you'd been burning down the predators ever since. You answered maybe five personal ads a week and most of the idiots on the other sides of these things disappeared when your undercover persona—Shannon—told them you were thirteen years old. Some stayed around until her fourth or fifth picture before they got nervous and disappeared. Every once in a while, though, maybe once a month, someone would hang on and push further, deeper into their fantasy.

And there you were for them and their fantasy: great at sounding like thirteen-year-old girl or a ten-year-old boy or a mother with twin tweener daughters looking for extra income. You knew how to be coy and draw the bad guys in, and sometimes you felt like history's greatest snake handler, charming the snakes until they were crawling all over you.

"Hey," your Deputy Chief asked, popping his head into your office.

"Chief," you said, surprised. "The hell you doing in on the weekend? Mama throw you out 'cause you kept wanting to add a goat to your sex life?"

He shook his head. "Oh, my God, you freak. Where do you get this crap?"

"I've seen pic—"

He raised a hand. "Stop. Don't want to hear it. Did you get the times on the community thing at the church in a couple of weeks?"

"Yeppers," you said. "Already in my calendar. Internet safety and parental empowerment?"

"That's my boy." He nodded at your undercover computer. "Got a new project?"

"Always."

He shook his head, always a little bemused and a little horrified. His face clouded in memory. Thirty years on the department, scrabbled up to the number-two position and he'd been involved in everything this department had handled for all of those years. He'd been the first officer on the scene, both when Shannon went missing and then when she'd been found.

Your insides tightened. When you saw his face that cloudy, you knew what he was about to ask.

"Think about her much?"

You took a deep breath, let your eyes linger on his. "All the time, Chief. She's never too far away. A cliché to say she's why I'm here, but—"

"But she's why you're here."

"Yeah," you said.

"Sometimes I imagine her talking to me."

"So do I," you said. "But you know the shit of it? I can't even remember what our last conversation was. I walked her home but I have no idea what we talked about."

His grin sat sideways on his face. "Yeah, probably nothing important. I wish we could have gotten the guy."

"Pussy State's Attorney didn't have balls enough to go on it. Case was too thin."

"Yeah, well." He stared at nothing for a few seconds. "Have a good night. Good luck."

When he was gone, you popped open each and every email from Daddy Commander and looked for any non-anonymous bit of digital information that took the man out of the realm of invisible.

to naughty? ain't no such thing as to naughty. we'll see. and if you are to nauhgty, then ill teach you a lesson. ropes and spanking and whatever else I can think of. email daddy back now.

"Nice grammar," you said as you popped open his second email.

what a cute girl. young and ripe.

And the third: *does your friend have more pictures we can play with?*

This was him dancing around the picture of Shannon. Telling you he thought it was a put on because that was the safest thing if anyone ever saw these emails, but also asking you, subtly, if this picture was really you.

The next few emails were longer, filling in puffy details about himself, getting all swole up to convince both of you he was something more than a piece of shit, maybe even almost human.

i own a construction company, he wrote. *very successful. some of the bigest buildings in chicago. tall skyscrapers. big like my cock. want to see my cock, little girl? i know you do. see it and touch it and suck it.*

Shocking to your non-cop friends but no surprise here. The real players always moved the conversation to sex damned quick, no art or nuance. This wasn't about romance, though most men tried to convince your undercover Shannon that every word and breath dripped romance.

This was sex. Mechanical. Pedestrian. Rocks off and move on to the next.

Which was exactly what you wanted it to be about; sex and getting their rocks off because that was the straightest line to prison.

Shannon's guy never went to prison, did he? Never even arrested so what the fuck does that get you?

Shannon's killer had slipped away when the TV news coverage started, when people started walking by his house and yelling, throwing eggs and toilet paper and then rocks and bricks. Quickly those thrown items became handmade yard signs calling him a pedophile. You watched it all, a scared and furious twelve-year-old who was angry the cops couldn't do anything to help the best girl you ever knew.

"So here I am," you said.

Here you am...nailing those bastards, Shannon said.

The next email: *your daddy is 35 years old and how old are you? youre picture looks 12 or 13. daddy is married but she is a bitch, doesn't understand me at all. a prude to. hates sex and wont fuck me at all. youll change that wont you? email me back and tell me all the things you want to do to me. I have a list of what ill do*

The rest of his emails got shorter as the minutes passed. He was getting antsy waiting for your responses. In one or two emails, he started to get angry but he quashed that fairly quickly.

He's been around, you think. *He's driven playmates away by getting angry.*

More and more emails, shorter and shorter. They left pretense behind and embraced all-sex-all-the-time. Asked Shannon questions about what she had done, what she wanted to do, what she knew, explaining exactly how he likes this and that. But through all the emails, he signed off "Daddy," kept his real name hidden. Gave nothing away.

"Damn it."

Until the last email. Too amped up by that point, probably whacking his Johnson as he typed one-handed, desperate to hear some word from you. In that last email, he screwed up.

where is little girl? daddy misses her. he has needs that have to be taken care of. and he hopes she is to naughty too be tied up. email youre daddy at HardBoppinDaddy@jetmail.com.

Bingo.

Now—Sunday, 2:34 a.m.

"I'm Jesse," says the counter man. He's got a single eye, the second covered by a black patch with skull and crossbones on it.

"Fuck him, I'm Jessie," says the woman. She's wearing a wife-beater, a smock over that, covered with grease and food stains. Her hands are gigantic and her fingers easily and comfortably play around the hilt of a carving knife.

Eye Man takes your money, quick and easy and gone before you realize it, as the woman slides three chalupas, rice, and a soda your way. Muerte comes from behind the counter and shoves a brown bag in the small of your back.

"They call me Jesse," he says.

"They call me—" you start to say.

"We're all of us Jesse." Muerte eyes you hard, squeezes your bicep in his giant hand. "Kill good, *pasma*."

You cross the street quickly, the food steaming inside a container. You see no one, as though the street cleared as soon as they handed you the daily special. No one left, no voices, even the gunshots, so constant on this part of Halsted Street, a condition of living in southside Chicago, have stopped.

They're all waiting on you, you think. *Waiting to see what you will do, to see if you have the balls to do the work...the wet work.*

"I do," you say.

The homeless man laughs. "Getting married? Gotta practice your lines?" His face lights up. "Brought me some tacos? I'll marry you for that. I'd'a preferred some smack but tacos..."

You glance at the container, then at him. "Chalupas."

"Even better, bitch." Grabbing them, he rips the container open. The first is gone instantly, the second more slowly.

He's digging into the third when you head to your car, a block over. When you're inside, you look at the daily special;

16

the brown bag Muerte stuffed into your waist. It's a Kimber 1911 and it surprises you. Usually, that's a beautiful weapon, but this is crappola. It's dented and dinged, the plastic Pachmayr grips are cracked, one of them missing completely. The sight is gone and the hammer is bent slightly to the left. The chrome is missing in two places.

"What a piece of shit," you say.

A drop gun, the kind of thing your fellow cops carry sometimes. Hell, this thing might just as easily explode and leave you dead as solve your problem. You figure you'll get a quick knock, nothing more, probably not even more than a couple of shots before the fucking barrel falls off or the magazine dumps.

You call Ashlee. Answers instantly, wide awake in spite of the hour. You knew she'd been waiting for this call. "Got it."

She breathes deeply, full of relief but edged with tension. "Good. Now get this done. I want him out of our lives."

You sigh. One-on-one with these guys is so fucking exhausting. It is hard on you and anyone in your orbit: friends, lovers, wives.

"Out of our bed," she says.

Your hands shake. "Yeah."

"And maybe no more answering personal ads?"

Your jaw grinds until pain rocks your head. If the judge hadn't been asleep at the switch, this wouldn't be happening. More than 100 counts of possession of child pornography... fifteen counts of production and distribution...four local girls identified as victims. Dumbass judge who didn't understand the dynamics of child pornography or HardBoppinDaddy's resources gaveled off on a $100,000 bond—ten percent to apply—so the fuck walked outta the county clink with $10,000 and a few bucks in processing fees.

Didn't just disappear, though, did he? Didn't slip away like Shannon's killer tried to do, did he? No, no, no, had to make a bigger splash than that.

"Go finish this. Then come home to me and fuck me any

way you want."

You grin. She says this sometimes but you're never completely sure how far down the menu she'll let you go. "Blah blah blah," like you always tease her.

"*Any*...way you want."

Then she's gone and you're alone in the car and your resolve crumbles. This is not what you wanted. You didn't want to be a customer at the taco truck. But neither did you want to hear Shannon's voice in memory. You wanted to hear it in real time, telling you she loved you, that she wanted to marry you and have your children.

Oh, babe, I do love you, she says. *Dead or not, I do love you, and if I were here, I would marry you in a heartbeat and have as many children as you wanted.*

It's all bullshit, you know. It's something your head invents so your heart feels better and you can hide from the loneliness that has plagued your life.

Your phone text alert goes off. Inner Circle's music chicka-chicka-ing until they start singing, "Bad boys, bad boys, wha'cha gonna do? Wha'cha gonna do when they come for you?"

COMING FOR YOU.

You respond without thinking. COMING FOR YOU. SAY GOODBYE TO MAMA B/C YOU WON'T MAKE THE NIGHT.

Then—Last Monday, 11:42 a.m.

You spent Sunday night with Ashlee.

Five minutes after she signed off, she came out of the building and saw you parked next to her car. She knew the signal. She could get in or not. Just as when you saw her parked next to your car and the choice was yours. Tonight, she got in and you silently took her home. That night she calmed you, soothed the demons dancing in your soul. You coupled twice, once quickly with the heat of teenagers, once slowly with the residual heat of the old man you actually are. She was beautiful and tender and said all the right things and left silence where you needed it.

While late-morning sun prismed through the window, she dried off from her shower. Her eyes were interested and excited. "So tell me about it."

"Daddy/Daughter. Emailed him last night. Sent a picture."

"Which will either scare him away," she said.

"Sucked him in," you said. "He emailed back in less than a half hour."

"Anything good?"

You grinned. "Oh, yeah. Fourteen emails. An email address in the last one."

She stared at you, dumbfounded. "Are you serious? An email address? 'Hey, coppers, here I am.'"

"Could be fake. But between it and the IP logins at the ad service, I'll find him."

She bends over, brushing her hair out.

"All kinds of talk, all very romantic," you said.

"Bullshit," she said.

"Got to sex damned fast. Explaining the mysteries of sex, the pleasures of the world, the intricacies of intimacy. I wrote two subpoenas last night and emailed them to the State's Attorney. I'll call him today and we'll get moving."

"Texting him yet?"

You shook your head. "Hopefully he'll send me his number first."

"What was the ad?"

"'Come see Daddy, Daughter, and do exactly as he says. He will tie you up and you will answer his every command.'"

She stared at you, amused but not surprised that you could recite the ad word for word. She'd seen you do this before. It was part of what happened to you when a new possibility cropped up. "No ages."

"Nope."

"Which means he's open to minors."

"*Might* be open to minors." You taught her that. Most men who want to play daddy/daughter safely listed acceptable ages for the playmates they're advertising for...thirty to forty, or twenty-five to thirty or even eighteen and up. You'd never seen an ad that asked for minors but you had seen ads that don't mention an age at all. It was one of the clues; men didn't list the ages because they didn't want to age themselves out of their fantasy...didn't want to wade through emails from women who were too old. But by listing no age, they also had deniability.

"And your gut says?" she asked.

You smiled, hugged her and put your hand on her delicious ass. "My gut says what the hell is a beautiful, *young* woman like you doing hanging with an old man like me."

She went to her knees, "I dig geriatrics," and took you deep into her mouth.

Now—Sunday 2:53 a.m.

"Dumbass," you say.

Your bravado had been as false as the night is deep right now, as deep as the shit in which you find yourself because of him.

I know your secrets, he'd said. *And I will end you with them.*

You swallow, letting the car drive you. It's random for a while, lefts and rights, straight runs, doubling back. You have no idea where you're going.

Yeah, you do...backward.

Headed back to Shannon. Headed back to the last afternoon you saw her. School had been out for an hour and you were just hanging with her, joking and trying to work up the courage to ask her to the dance next week. You'd talked about it with her but hadn't been able to ask her directly. Titty baby...you'd already been roller skating with her and to a couple of baseball games and even Taste of Chicago last summer, but somehow this was different and the question stuck in your throat. She knew you wanted to ask. Laughed about it, teased you...gently... and danced around the question, trying to draw you out.

When you finally did, when your lips and tongue managed to give the words life in the warm air, her face went red and she nodded and the world changed.

"Fucking idiot," you say. "She's gone and you're gone and it's all gone." Going back to her over and over was just a shitty unfulfillable pipe dream. She was never going to be your wife and that's how it was.

You take a deep breath. You're stalling for time, you know. You don't want to text him again, you don't want to meet him. You don't want to kill him, but what other choice is there?

He has made it clear there is no reprieve. He's looking to burn you down.

Angry, at him, at the man who killed Shannon, maybe at Shannon herself for getting herself kidnapped, but mostly angry that your choice twenty-plus years ago put you on this street at night with an illegal weapon in your lap, you fire up your phone and send a text.

FUCK YOU. YOUR SUGAR DADDY IS GONE & NOTHING WILL BRING HIM BACK. WANT TO KILL ME BECAUSE HE MADE A CHOICE? THEN GET TO THE KILLING, BITCH.

You hit send and then turn on the GPS app and share it with him.

I'LL BE AT 'A' ST PARK

You check the load in the Kimber, start the car, and head for the denouement.

Then—Last Monday, 3:01 p.m.

That afternoon, Ashlee long since arisen from her knees, wiping her mouth, dressing, and taken back to her car while you went to work, you called the assistant State's Attorney.

"Yo, sexy," the man, Tom, said. "Hey, the grapevine is leaking all about you and a certain chickee. Doing some sparkin'?"

You chuckled. Can't keep shit secret in this department. Everyone's secrets were out there; the chief's personal armory paid for out of the department's drug fun, a commander's trips over the state line so no one saw that his dates didn't have that extra chromosome, a dispatcher's love of blood sport and attendance at cock fights; no secrets anywhere.

McCann stopped in your doorway, motioned you to the watch commander's office.

Speaking of secrets.

Rumors and conjecture. No one has seen him hit any of his wives, no one has ever seen him even yell at his women and ex-women.

At least he had marriages and ex-wives. Yours got stolen before you had a chance at it.

Shannon.

Your first love, the one woman no other woman has been able to compete against.

You understood the loneliness tearing at him, it tore at you, too. Eating that meal together is how you cooked so well together when you were shift mates, before his promotion to sergeant— good choice, he was a solid first line supervisor—and then his promotion to lieutenant—disastrous choice because his fucking fascist ego got promoted, too.

"Yo, dickhead," Tom said. "I'm talking here."

You snapped back to the phone. "And so wildly interesting your conversation always is, too. Sorry, I was wiping my butt so kinda forgot about you."

Tom laughed. "Ouch. I was saying, that Ashlee is quite a woman. Probably more than you can handle. Tell you what, when it falls apart, you send her my way and I'll show her a real man."

"You found one?" you asked.

There was a split second of silence, "Fucker," then he laughed. "Listen, I'm glad you called. The Briddick case."

"Yeah?" You tightened up.

"Evidentiary hearing is coming up. I never got the email attachments from after he was arrested."

There is no need to dredge through your memory; Briddick was front and center. The arrest was six months ago. "*When* he was arrested, not after. Briddick was downloading the attachments as we came through the door."

In the phone, Tom snorted. "That's crazy shit, man. They must have been sent as you guys were gearing up to hit the door."

"Couldn't have been timed any better."

"Okay, so from what I remember, you told me those videos are the heaviest part of the case. The rest of it was not as strong?"

"Those videos *are* the case," you said. "That entire case was just a handful of photos until those videos came along."

"Well, I need those vids."

"Okay," you said. "You'll get them today."

"Great. Thanks. Now, what can I do for you?"

"Answered a new ad and—"

"*Cha ching*," Tom said. "Your cases are always money. Do tell."

"He emailed back like damn near instantly. Ripe and ready, I think. I emailed over some subpoenas. Any chance getting them today?"

"Right now, man. Got nothing else going on and the judge is free. Gimme like twenty minutes and I'll email them over."

You were surprised. Usually it took a couple of days to get them. "That's great. Thank you."

"No problem," Tom said. "Do us good, babe, and stay sexy."

McCann had his back to you when you stepped into the watch commander's office, the phone at his ear. "I hear you and I'll get it paid as soon as I can. When? I don't know. Next week? Week after? Yeah, yeah, fine, whatever." He slammed the phone down and saw you. Instantly, he plastered something like neutrality on his face. "Got a new one lined up?"

"News travels," you said.

"Can't let you detach from duty, we've got two out injured. So you'll have to reel in your new project while handling calls."

Disappointment wormed through you. These projects were so intense, it was easier to focus just on them. But you were an officer first and an online exploitation investigator second. You understood how the egg cracked.

"Two injured? What happened?"

When you left the night before, you had one copper out with a broken ankle. Shattered during a foot chase on an outside security gig.

"Mikey broke his hand last night. Guy didn't want to come to jail."

"Who of us does?" you asked.

McCann laughed but it was heavy and awkward and pointed. "Feel like I can't get out."

You sat. "I hear you, Loot. Them womens...they ain't worth the trouble." You declared it as though it's a universal truth.

He grin was empty and flat. "Yeah, they are."

Shannon.

"Yeah, they really are." Your head flooded with the scent and feel of Ashlee's touch, of her mouth and skin, how her eyes burned through you, how her whisper left you dizzy and hungry.

"This isn't my exes, though. Hell, that'd be easy: 'No more money...the well is dry!'" He laughed bitterly. "Just got caught a little short this month."

"The well's been dry a long time, Loot."

"Long as the fucking Sahara desert's been around." Distaste appeared in his eyes, bleeding down to his cheeks and over his crinkled lips. "So...this new project."

"He's ready to go. Emailed me about eleventy-hundred times last night. He'll send me his digits today and we'll be off to the races. Already got two subpoenas. Should have them sent within the next hour."

McCann shook his head. "Moving quick."

"Like putting bad guys away."

His phone dinged and he checked the text. Instantly, as though someone had changed the channel or snapped off a light, his body relaxed. His face smoothed and his breathing eased.

"Bro comes through again? Good to have someone to prime that well."

He glared. No one else knew about his half-brother and he hated having it brought up. It was a humiliating piece of his life, reduced by ex-wives and children and bad stock market choices and the harsh mistress of debt to taking monthly handouts from a man who made millions with video screens that spewed twenty-four-hour news channels and ads for airport eateries and boutiques and newsstands, who'd sold that company at age fifty and hadn't worked a day since.

You had met Jonathon a few times when you and Terry were shift mates and holy balls did you know *exactly* where li'l bro Terry had gotten his harsh streak of control freakishness and you suspected Jonathon's piles and piles and oodles of money did that to him. It was all about perception with Jonathon and having a younger brother so sloppy as to have three ex-wives with a fourth working on that title had to get beneath his blue-blooded skin. So he let the money flow from his account to Terry's because blood will out every time, but you were certain he made Terry's life shit-worthless over it.

"Hey, man," you said. "We all have bears to cross."

"Keep Jon outta your mouth. Do your job—" He stopped

and you could see him hanging on by his fingertips. He wanted to lash out. "Get out of my office." His jaw ground hard. "Get the fuck out."

Now—Sunday, 3:07 a.m.

You told him the park.

It's five blocks away and it has a name, somebody's name, but everyone refers to it as 'A' Street Park. It's shaped like a splash of water, curving this way and that, a smallish native plant sanctuary dropped in the middle, four or five different street access points, solar lights along the walking path, trees with nattering squirrels, and a view of the lake on the north side while houses guarded the south and west side; nice neighborhoods of upper middle class citizens who constantly called when suspicious people were in *their* park.

Yet they had never called about Jameson P. Andrews, had they? By the time you arrested him, in that park, for trading massive amounts of child pornography, he'd been in the park taking pictures and videos of young kids for the better part of two years.

He was your first arrest when you began this sexploitation journey. A peer-to-peer trading arrest and you were scared to death. You moved so slowly, making certain everything was perfect and had the backing of the State's Attorney and two different judges. When you finally executed the search warrant you had an entire tactical team standing by just in case Andrews did something crazy.

You didn't know, did you? Your first bust, your first time dealing with child porn bad guys. You had no idea what to expect.

By now, headed to the park where you'd busted so many bad guys, you had a damned good idea of what to expect. You knew them, more intimately than you'd ever had expected. It was a disgusting knowledge, one that left you standing in steaming hot showers until your skin puckered red.

"I know how it is," you said to them, constant variations on a single theme. "Look at her. She's a whore, dressing like a nine-year-old whore."

"Yeah, this is her fault."

"Sure, it is. They know how to dress, they know how to walk and look. Winking and smiling like bitches. They don't learn that shit at college? Hell, no, Mama teaches 'em in elementary school."

A bit of that; push a little here, pull a little there, and every single one of them opened up and told you all about how it was the girls in the pictures who caused them to trade, caused them to touch themselves and eventually touch new victims. You knew how to get them to confess and the knowledge disgusted you and made you keep turning up the heat on those showers until your skin puckered blood red and once even blistered.

Jameson P. Andrews's arrest had gone soft and easy, no violence, no resisting.

Exactly how HardBoppinDaddy's arrest had gone.

You'd had the full team surrounding the house but it had been you and Ashlee who'd approached the door and knocked. The computer forensics guys had been in their smoked-window black SUVs half a block down.

You knocked, HardBoppinDaddy answered and knew instantly who you were.

"You're Shannon." Said with resignation but shot through with a trembling anger.

"Yes," you had said.

He nodded acknowledgement, allowed you in, and sat exactly where you told him to. Everyone else spread through the house to begin collecting electronics. But you sat with him, mirandized him, and tried to do your thing.

"Save your breath," he'd said, and gone dead silent, staring at the wall and never moving a muscle.

"Hey," Ashlee had said. She'd taken you to the garage, located in the back of the house, looking out over a drive that emptied into the alley.

In that garage, HardBoppinDaddy's wheels. A silver BMW. Two bags packed and tossed into the passenger seat, one of them had fallen to the footwell.

Then she had taken you deeper in his house, to his office; his computer. Smashed until it looked like a frost covering the floor, computer grey in hundreds of tiny shards, cables sliced, the monitor with a single ball-peen hammer blow that gave it the look of a pirate; a single eye.

"The hell'd he know we were coming?" Ashlee had asked.

Seven hours later the electronics had been cracked open and there had been no secrets to see. Every device had been empty. Clean and empty of contraband.

You had tried to move quick—getting the subpoenas and then a search warrant—but hadn't been quick enough, and through it all, HardBoppinDaddy had never made a sound.

About forty-six hours later, a judge set bail, HardBoppin-Daddy posted it, climbed in a cab and disappeared. He hadn't been seen since.

Just like Shannon's guy.

Which gets us to tonight, doesn't it, Shannon asks.

"Nothing I haven't done before."

She laughs, the little girl laugh you knew all through elementary school, the one that always accompanied a red face and hands curled beneath her chin. She says, *Gangsta.*

"No."

You keep driving, the park only a few minutes from here. Holding a death grip on that gun, your entire body flying at the power in that grip, at the metal extension of...*you.*

Superman, she says.

"No," you say as the terrible screech of car brakes shatters the silence.

You look up and see his car blast out of the alley, thunder to a stop in front of you.

"Son of a bitch," you say.

He grins and levels a gun at you.

Then—Last Monday, 7:14 p.m.

HEY LITTLE GIRL IS THIS U

Sent your number two minutes ago and now the alert tone you use for sexual predators dinged.

If HardBoppinDaddy was standard Chesta Molesta, he would send a batch of texts, then a couple minutes would pass, then he'd send a batch more. Those spaces between were filled, you knew, with him texting other girls. Your first ad arrest had texted fourteen girls at once.

And sure as shit, it turns out HardBoppinDaddy was just another low-rent Chesta Molesta, and yeah, he spewed text messages at you. But the best part? The number with these texts? Daddy Commander's phone number? A 312-area code.

Downtown Chicago.

You responded: YEAH DADDY THIS IS ME

HOW R U 2DAY

GOOD SLEPT GOOD LAST NIGHT DREAMING

DREAMING OF DADDY OF WHAT DADDY WILL DO 2 U

...

...LOST IT WHEN I WAS 12 LITTLE GIRL. SUMMER BETWEEN 7TH AND 8TH GRADE R U STILL A VIRGIN...

...

...KISSED A BOY A FEW TIMES BUT MOSTLY NOTHING ELSE. ;) I'M JUST 13 SILLY MAN...

...

...NAW UR NOT 2 BUEATIFUL 2 B 13. DO U HAVE PICTURES 2 PROVE IT?

WHAT KIND OF PICTURES?

UR BUEAITUFL FACE MY LOVE LETS START THERE

You snorted. "My love," slipped in nice and gentle. Trying to convince you this was all love and he's the only one who understands you, that you can trust him with anything.

You shot him a pic quick.

Is that how he did it, Shannon? Did you learn to trust him? Learn to let him in to your most secret places, the parts of your soul you showed no one...not even me?

Almost immediately: THANK U 4 THE PIC. DO U HAVE ANYMORE? PLAYING WITH UR DOGGIE OR HOP-SCOTCH OR SOEMTHING

HOPSCOTCH? SILLY MAN THAT'S A KIDDIE THING I'M GROWN UP

GROWN UP HUH? PROVE IT

So you sent the beach picture; Shannon in a swimsuit. Silent for twenty minutes and you knew what was up. Tried not to see a fat middle-aged guy hammering his crank and spilling lube all over the chair.

"PPD-10."

Damnit, not now.

You keyed your portable radio. "Go ahead."

"10-25 Sidetracked bar...subject removal."

You hoped to get in and out fast. Usually subject removal calls were done quick. The subject needing removal left of their own accord because they didn't want a beef with the cops.

Not this time. This time, the guy stayed in the bar and wanted to fight and your back up was on a traffic crash and so after talking for twenty minutes you said, "Fuck it," and Tased the shit outta the guy when he ran at you with a pool cue.

EMTs, arrest, transport, booking paperwork at the jail, report after that. All told, Daddy Commander/HardBoppinDaddy was without you for nearly four hours.

The moment you were free you blasted back to your office and yanked the undercover phone out. Lots of texts, getting angrier by as each unanswered second passed.

LITTLE GIRL UR PISSING DADDY THE FUCK OFF

You frowned. Never been down this road before. No one had gotten angry, they'd just slipped away into the cybernight and found themselves other victims. This guy radiated anger, rage between every word and each character.

You leaned back in your chair. These projects were a matter of balance: the right amount of this, not too much of that. Keeping the suspects headed the direction you needed them to go, that they wanted to go, without them realizing who you were.

"Reel him back in," you said. "Set that hook again."

You sent him the roller-skating picture, a nice shot of Ashlee from behind. You've cropped it subtly, just enough to move the focal point slightly from the two smiling girls to Ashlee's rear end.

You read his last text as you sent it.

DONT PISS DADDY OFF YOU WONT LIKE WHAT HAPPENS

Now—Sunday 3:16 a.m.

His car bullets from the alley, skids to a halt directly in front of you. You hammer the brakes, getting your car stopped just before it slams into his.

Should'a pounded it and killed him.

Drill that fucker right in the ass and sent him knocking on Scratch's inferno.

He's not surprised to see you, that he came across your car. You can see it in every line of his doughy face.

Dumbass, you think.

You'd shared GPS with him. In your anger and bravado, you'd told him exactly where you were. Your brain, thick with rage and grief, had wanted to tell him where to meet you and show him on the GPS app.

Maybe what you wanted, but not what you did.

Now he was following you, probably paralleling you a block over, watching and waiting for you to hit a red light or thick traffic or whatever. And when he saw it? Fucker blasted over and now...what?

Bullet to the face? Or five or six to the chest? Maybe drag you out of the car and run your ass over ten or fifteen times.

"Son of a bitch," you say.

That goofy, almost maniacal grin you've seen before. He's talking, too; indistinguishable words lost behind two windshields, his anger, and your fear. You can't hear his words but you can sure as shit see them.

Then his gun is on you. Twenty feet away, maybe thirty, but feels as though it's right here, in the car with you, crowding you, threatening you—killing you.

"I'm sorry, Shannon, I tried."

Shut the hell up, she shouts. *Go! Go now!*

You hammer the accelerator and your car leaps forward.

Surprise and fear bleeds from his face when you smash into him, metal shrieking as his car spins halfway around. He twists around in the driver's seat, trying to find you as you back up, prepare for another run.

Drive by, you think. His plan is a cheap drive by. He wants this to look like some random banger decided to pop you.

"Stupid shit," you shout at him, your voice straining over the screech of your tires. "Doesn't solve your problem."

In his head, this was the quick solution. Leave you dead and him clean and clear.

Your car fishtails, bangs against a curb, then a couple of trash cans, straightens out for a moment, then fishtails again as you round a corner. His headlights burst into your rearview and stab your eyes like ice picks. Panic begins, down in the deepest part of your core; a panic you've felt before.

Take a breath, Shannon says. *We'll be fine.*

"This isn't about we, god damn it," you shout at her, yanking the wheels right and back left, trying to stay on the road. "This is me. I'm dying here. He's really going to do this." You slam your hand against the steering wheel, over and over, until blood spatters your face, warm and wet. There is no pain, washed out in fear.

Shannon is gone, her lack of presence, her absence, is palpable. It is a gaping black hole in your universe.

"Shannon, I'm sorry. Please."

Silence answers you.

Punctuated by gunshots. Two. Three. One bullet shatters your back windshield. Another thunks the trunk.

This isn't problem solving, you think. This isn't even the reckoning. This is simple revenge.

Another shot tears through the seat and into—and out of— your shoulder.

You feel nothing. Maybe it's adrenaline, maybe it's because you're so fucking tough, but either way, there is nothing. Blood spatters to the dashboard, runs off the windshield. It's curious, more than a bit weird, but that's all. Something to be seen rather than felt, something to be questioned rather than screamed over.

You glance at the gun, the Kimber 1911. *How many bodies on this gun*, you wonder.

"One more doesn't mean shit."

You round another corner, eyes digging in hard at all the traffic. Cops? Pedestrians? You push the car faster, banging up over fifty now on a narrow residential street. The headlights behind you fall back a bit, weave more than yours do.

He's reloading.

His headlights are a knife stabbing from the dark, looking for you, and now there is pain seeping into your consciousness from your shoulder. You take a quick glance, scared to take your eyes off the road too long as the needle creeps past sixty.

Checking the Kimber's magazine, seeing they only gave you five rounds and nothing in the chamber, you say, "I love you, Shannon."

Another shot blasted through your car.

Slamming into a parked truck, bouncing off the curbs five or six more times, wiping the sweat from your face, you manage to rack a round into the chamber of the Kimber, and yank the wheel hard left.

"Follow me down a little further, asshole," you say.

The headlights behind you turn with you.

Then—Last Wednesday, 7:45 a.m.

You soothed Daddy Commander's anger through Tuesday night and into Wednesday morning. He finally stopped texting about 6:30 a.m. and you assumed he fell asleep. The length of that session was nothing new; you'd had bad boys text for eighteen or twenty or twenty-two hours straight. When you signed off Wednesday morning, you were exhausted but exhilarated, almost giddy at having saved the entire case.

FAV COLOR

FAV SHAPE

WHAT KIND OF PANTIES

WEARING A BRA YET

EVER TOUCHED A BOY

All separate texts, in and around nearly 500 other texts; the sexual but also the mundane. Homework, favorite classes, what school Shannon went to, what her grades were.

She went to school with me, you thought. You downed a quick blast of orange juice and headed to bed. From first grade until she was murdered in the seventh grade and her killer walked away. How many times had you seen that son of a bitch after he killed her? Strutting through the mall or washing his car at that janky little place over on Black Road near Infantry Street? Or walking along her street, passing the house where Shannon's parents still grieved, his face smug and superior?

Shannon had been, at least in your nostalgic head, the perfect woman and that bastard had stolen her before either she or you realized that perfection.

"Focus, you idiot," you said.

Sometimes, you had to let the texts go unanswered for a couple hours. The slipstream was so intense, 24/7 if the bad guys could get it, and they were all-sex, all-the-time. The sheer temperature of the fire, an overheating smelter, burned away your soul and left nothing but charred remains. Taking breaks from these guys, connecting with Ashlee or sitting in the dark and talking to Shannon, was the only way to cool the flames.

At other times, you bombarded the target; every random thing a little girl might be thinking at any given time. You tried to make it as intense for them as they made it for you, and as often as you could, you worked in a reminder that Shannon was thirteen years old.

Through that eighteen hours with HardBoppinDaddy, you did the same thing. Gave him multiple opportunities to get out of the coming shitstorm.

13 HUH WELL 2 ME AGE IS JUST A NUBMER IT DONT MEAN ANYTHING

You answered him: NO IT DOESN'T.

I LUV U, he texted.

I LOVE U, TO.

By 2:30 a.m. Wednesday, it was time for the big hook: Shannon's story. You live with Gramma. So many damned rules, drives you nutty. She doesn't trust you at all and you hate it. You need some freedom, some space to do whatever you might want to do. You gave him some laughing emojis and told him that you weren't really a naughty girl, in spite of what your email said. You were a good girl but a friend dared you to answer the ad.

I LIKE THE PICTURES OF UR DOGIES.

I LIKE ALL THE PLACES U BEEN

I LIKE ALL YOUR BUILDINGS...THERE SO BIG AND TALL

You told him maybe Gramma would take you downtown to see his buildings sometime and you know the subtle references to his phallus drove him berserk.

IS UR WIFE REALLY A BITCH?

SHE IS

SHE WON'T HAVE SEX WITH U AT ALL?

SHE WON'T

IVE NEVER HAD SEX. TOUCHED A BOY ONCE. IS THAT SEX?

NO, LOVE ILL TEACH U DO U WANT ME 2 TEACH U

A BOY GRABBED MY BOOB AT THE MOVIES ONCE. SQUEEZED SO HARD IT MADE ME CRY. IT HURT BAD.

I WOULD NEVER HURT U LITTLE GIRL U R THE EX-ACT WOMAN IVE ALWAYS LOOKED 4 ALL I WANT 2 DO IS LUV U

I KNOW SILLY MAN U WOULD NEVER HURT ME U TREAT ME LIKE A PRINCES NO ONE DOES

Your personal phone rang and Ashlee's name crawled across the screen.

"Hey, babe," you said.

"Chickee baby." Her voice was smooth. "You're up."

"Haven't gone down yet."

She growled. "Son of a bitch. It's 7:45. You gotta get some sleep."

"I hear you." Her car radio crackled in the background. "Are you on duty?"

She snorted. "Got called for a day shift. Overtime so I'm on the big clock. Listen, I saw Tom headed in to the SA's office a few minutes ago. You got some subpoena returns first thing this morning. He gave them to me."

"Yeah?" Excitement tickled your belly. That was quick and it was the information you always started with: who was this guy? Where did he live? His texts and emails gave you the when and why of the search warrant you'd already started writing, his electronics the what, but the information in those subpoenas returns would give you the who and where.

Who. What. When. Where. Why. The how explicit in the IP address logins.

"Jet Mail?" you asked her.

"Jet Mail and Flip both. Tom got them via email so he forwarded those to you."

"Pop open my department mail, see what it says. I can't wait until I sign on at two."

She whistled. "Hey, man, that's a big step, isn't it? I mean, moving in together is one thing but *this*? Your department email password?"

You grinned. You guys hadn't talked about shacking up together at all, but it was a nice bit of funny. "Yeah, that's probably true."

"Gimme your password."

"Asterisk 66 capital AB lower case B capital A forward slash backward slash number 7 number 3 lower case Q."

Her laugh made you grin. "What the fuck is that?"

"Tamper proof."

"What the hell ever." She went silent for a second. "ABBA. Unbelievable. You probably secretly listen to them, don't you?"

"Not so secretly."

"Can't believe I got involved with you."

"Well, me either, actually. Someday you'll come to your senses."

"Probably not. The emails from Jet Mail and Flip are just links."

"Right. They go to secure sites so I can download the information confidentially. Go ahead."

You heard her banging around on the keys. "Boom! We got a name. Frances J. Hudson."

You whispered the name to yourself a few times, tasting the perversion on your tongue.

"Jet Mail has an account recovery email and phone number. Flip has...hang on. Flip has no name but an email address listed."

"And it is?"

She pauses. "HardBoppinDaddy@jetmail.com."

You had him and the tingle in your belly grew to straight up excitement.

"Same phone number," she said. "Flip and Jet Mail both have the same phone number listed."

"And it is?"

She rattled off the number, a 312-area code and it is the exact number that's been texting you from Daddy Commander.

"That's it." You heard her excitement. "That's him. You got him, babe."

"Well, getting closer. Tell me this: are there IP logins listed?"

She hesitated. "Lots of number-dot-number-dot blah blah."

You laughed. "You are a technical wizard, aren't you?"

"Not my job. That's all you, dude. Yeah, there are IPs all over the place on both returns."

Those would be the next step. Subpoena the internet service provider, get a trail from Hudson through the IP address to Jet Mail and the Flip ad, even as you used that same IP trail and phone number to track him from his phone to you.

"Do me a favor. Read through Flip and tell me what all he's been doing."

For a few seconds, there was dead silence; a disbelief you could clearly hear.

"Ash?"

"Holy balls." She swallowed. "Flip says he's had...hang on." She counted, mostly quietly but whispering sometimes. "Crap-'a'mighty...he's had fifty-three ads in the last six months."

Your heart squeezed you, almost stopped. "Fifty-three?" How many little girls—little Shannons—did that mean?

"Fuck yeah. For everything. Women *and* men. Got a taste for dark meat, too. Couple ads for fat chicks. A couple for trannies. Sometimes wants to be dominant, sometimes wants to be submissive. Tops, bottoms. Man, this dude is into everything."

You frowned. None of that sounded like a man fixated on young girls. "What about Daddy/Daughter?"

"Just the one you answered."

To you, to your experience, that sounded like a man getting into something new. "How many responses to it?"

"Four, I think, kinda hard to read this stuff. Will all those girls have to be interviewed?"

41

"Well, they might not all be young girls. Probably adult women wanting to play."

"Man, that shit's just weird."

Her car radio crackled. "PPD-27 from dispatch. Criminal trespass to property."

"Go play copper," you said to Ashlee.

"Yep. Get some sleep before your shift, okay, babe?"

"Hah! Not going to happen. Time to write. More subpoenas and a search warrant."

"Damnit, babe. Get some sleep. Want me to come over tonight after you get off?"

"That sounds nice. Maybe a pizza or something."

"Emphasis on something," she said.

After hanging up, you cranked open your department email and read more closely what she had just given you. More than ninety percent of the logins were the same IP address, a single company. You chose five random login IPs, then five more specific to when he posted the ad and when he'd answered Shannon's emails. You keep subpoena templates in your Drafts folder so you popped one open, inserted the IP addresses, dates, times UTC. Within twenty minutes of Ashlee's phone call, you had emailed a new subpoena to Tom.

"Yo, twinkle butt," you said when he answered the phone.

He laughed. "I thought maybe getting some returns would get your juices flowing. This one is moving fucking fast, isn't it?"

"Faster than you realize. If you check your email, you'll see a new subpoena."

He whistled. "Dude, you are a machine. So there's a YouTube video of John Bonham. From Led Zeppelin?"

"Duh."

"There's an isolated drum track of 'Fool in The Rain.' Ever hear it?"

"Uh...no. You're the only freak I know who's freakish enough to listen to isolated drum tracks."

"Well, whatever. The point is, reminds me of you. Bonham is

relentless in that thing. Just keeps going. That's you, man. Relentless."

"Whatevs. Listen, I've got the search warrant template done. It's all filled in except the last couple of subparagraphs tying him to his service provider. That's the subpoena I sent just now. Soon as I get that info, I'll be ready to go in front of a judge."

"Relentless," Tom said as he hung up.

You turned back to the returns and read through them, much more slowly and carefully, making sure you missed nothing.

"I'm coming for you, buddy," you said, making some raspberry hot chocolate.

Frances J. Hudson, Daddy Commander, HardBoppinDaddy.

Hell, yeah, you are, Shannon said. *Just like you did my guy.*

No, you think. *Not like that. Better than that. Frances J will rot in prison forever.*

Now—Sunday, 3:29 a.m.

Deep in the industries now; small and medium factories, smoke probably belching but invisible in the night sky except where it blotted the stars out.

Driving fast, too fast, skidding out of residential neighborhoods and onto work alleys and broken-down delivery roads. In and out of gravel entryways, leaving car paint against metal Dumpsters, bits of tire rubber all over everything. Wheel barely under your control, your hands soaked in sweat, your shoulder screaming from the shot, the pain long since chewed through your adrenaline.

He stays with you, though, and it infuriates you, though it also burns your throat with fear. He matches you turn for turn, block for block. Every break you caught, every time you managed to leave him behind by a few yards or even a half a block, he found a way to slip back into you. Nothing helps you, nothing slows him.

"This is bullshit," you say to no one.

You've been a copper for more than fifteen years, on the road the entire time, and you're not a fan of EVO driving. Code 3, lights and siren, blasting through stop signs and traffic lights, praying to God people stay out of your way. Now your busting EVO in a personal car, no lights or siren, no hopped-up tranny or suspension system, just a standard, early-model, previously owned Acura. You hate emergency vehicle operations but now you wish you'd paid attention better, had better control of this fucking Acura.

Control the car better? Fuck that, you wish you had better control of *everything* that was happening.

Better control of everything since Shannon disappeared.

He shoots again and you howl. Bullets wang off your car, deflect into other cars and through windows and why the Christ hasn't anyone called the cops yet?

You yank the wheel hard right, hop the curb and kill a mailbox. Around a streetlight post but the screech along your rear quarter panel tells you it's probably coming down. With any fucking luck, it'll come down on him, crash through his skull, trail pieces of him for a half block before his car stops.

Another shot. And another. Thunk thunk and then—The car is out of control. The frontend dancing back and forth, and you realize the left side is lower, bouncing hard. He hit a tire and you see sparks start to fly.

The rim gouges in the road, louder than your fear and even your scream. It catches on a curb or a rain catch basin or God alone knows what and spins your car. The Kimber slides around, disappears into the passenger wheel well. Too far away.

"Fuck fuck fuck!"

He smashes into your rear, jamming you into two or three parked cars, and you're not going anywhere.

Silence pounds the both of you as you both step out and stare at each other.

"I do love a good chase," he says. "Always did. Remember our first one? The rapist? Did his girlfriend, then stole her car and took off?"

"That was a long time ago."

He yanks his gun up, dead on you, just as you raise, dead on him. You stare at each other, aimed at each other, both ready to kill.

"We were shift mates once," McCann says. "Guess those days are over."

As though your gun hands are tied together, Battle Royale, you each move to your right, spinning around a central point.

"Yeah, you motherfucker, those days are over."

Then—Last Wednesday, 11:57 p.m.

"Get your ass in here." McCann's voice boomed like an explosion, shattering walls and shaking the ceiling.

You were in the hallway, just finished the report on the DUI arrest that had you here late.

"Now!"

You felt the anger heating your blood. Lieutenant or not, you and McCann had once been shift mates and treating you like that was egotistical bullshit. You both had stripes and scars from all the wars so who the fuck was he to order you around like you were some rookie? You had fought one of your local idiots for twelve and a half minutes when he got control of McCann's gun; you had popped the church arsonist together. When his second wife left and then everything started going south with his third wife, who did he come to?

"What the hell is your problem?" you said, striding into his office.

He whirled, face full of the anger of the universe. He shoved his visitor's chair out of the way to get to you, his hands up and grabbing. He tripped over the chair's leg, stumbled, came up yelling and cursing, his face was red, sweaty, his entire body aggressive and demanding. "What the fuck are you doing?"

"Whoa...*whoa*," you said, putting a hand up to stop him.

"Don't you fucking touch me." Spittle flew from his lips. He was a foot away from you, filling your personal space, trying to crowd you, trying to push you backward to put your back against the door frame. He reached around you, yanked the door closed so hard you waited for the glass to rain down.

He's never been like this before. At that moment, in that office, anger was the very air he breathed. Red and violent, a mist like that of a spring storm. His eyes were alive and enraged, his hands clenched. "I said, 'What the fuck are you doing?'"

You let a few seconds pass before you answered. "I have no idea what you're talking about."

He waved some papers in your face. "Your new one. Frances J. Hudson."

"What about him?" You thought back through the entire investigation. Had you missed something? Screwed something up? Made an assumption that turned out to be wrong?

"You're leading this target, dumbass. The State's Attorney wants to shut the entire thing down."

You side-stepped, not out of fear of McCann, but out of confusion. Leading Hudson? You couldn't even wrap your head around what McCann was saying. Nothing you'd talked about with HardBoppinDaddy had been your suggestion, everything—every single word—was his. He led you; took Shannon's hand and led her down the same well-worn path all your bad guys travelled. There was nothing different here so why was McCann losing his shit?

"I am not leading anyone. I'll get you the transcripts."

"I've read the transcripts."

You stared, confusion riding thick in your head. He's read them? How the hell did that work? You've downloaded nothing, printed nothing, transferred nothing. "You what?"

"Read them, and I gotta tell you, this is the sloppiest investigation I've ever seen. You're leading him. Lying about who you are."

"Of course I'm lying about who I am, that's how this is done."

"God damn it, stop patronizing me. You've gone beyond what a cop can lie about. This case is dead so end it."

"End it? What the hell—Are you stupid?"

He sputtered, his face gone crimson and his hands clenched to tight fists. He was barely in control, wanting to go hands on right then and there. "That's insubordination. You're suspended. As of now."

"What the hell is going on? My investigation is fine, I'm not leading anyone, I'm not sloppy on anything. And unless you've hacked my undercover account, you haven't read any transcripts. No one at the State's Attorney's Office wants this closed down."

His was suddenly quiet and calm. "Did you just call me a liar?"

"No," you said. "I said you were mistaken, that someone at the SA's office told you incorrectly and led you to believe some bullshit. And you can't suspend me, Terry, only the Chief and Deputy Chief can and then only after an investigation of my supposed crime."

"I can do what I feel is in the best interest—"

"No, you can't and we both know it." You lowered your voice, tried to project calm, and righted the chair he'd thrown out of the way to get to you. You sat, looking toward his desk rather than behind you at him, and waited.

Eventually, he sat, eyes the color of molten steel. "I will forward my report to the Chief and you should contact your union representative."

"Fuck all that," you shook your head dismissively. "I don't care about that. What is going on here...with you? Why are you so pissed off at me?"

"You screwed up this new project...this Daddy Commander HardBoppinDaddy whatever. Fucked it up completely."

"No, I didn't. What's going on?"

"You killed your case."

"No, I didn't. Terry, what's going on?"

"Drop the case, damn it." He took a deep breath. "Just stop it cold, file a report that says he finally decided you were a cop and so got out of it, and I'll try my hardest to keep official misconduct charges off of you."

Lie? In a report? You swallowed, wiped the sweat off your head. *Official misconduct?*

"Do what I'm telling you, save your career."

What in hell was playing out here? "Save my—my career is fine."

McCann leaned back, a smirk on his face. "You just couldn't

take it, could you? You were fine with my sergeant's promotion. Probably thought you'd get one pretty quick and we'd be the same level again."

"We were at the same level, in case you forgot. I got promoted, too."

"Took you awhile, though, didn't it? Had to eat my shit for two years, didn't you? Then I got my bars and it's killing you, ain't it? So you're doing anything you can to get ahead. Fix up crappy cases and hope command notices and promotes you."

You snorted. "Load of shit. You wanna climb the chain, have a grand old time. I couldn't care less about how hard you suck that chain. But I'll tell you this...right now, with this...this...crap, you're proving exactly why your promotion was bullshit."

"Drop this investigation."

"Is that an order?"

"Yes."

"Then kiss my ass."

He smiled and said, "That's insubordination...again."

"Kiss my ass, sir."

He tapped a manila folder sitting on his desk with a single finger. "You been here a long time. You know this place, man."

"Meaning?"

"All the secrets come out."

You said nothing, fear tickling your balls. You tried to keep your face neutral and uninterested.

"No one can hide their secrets. This particular secret? Gotta say...it surprised the shit outta me."

Panic exploded in you, an acid dumped down your throat, swallowed by the gallon, mainlined, and eating you instantly. Your muscles suddenly hurt, your brain was thick, shutting down.

He knows, Shannon said.

No, he doesn't, you told yourself. This isn't happening, can't happen, he knows nothing. Nobody knows. I'm not an idiot, I didn't leave it out there for the world to find. Nobody knows anything. You took a deep breath, then a few more, and then tried to act as though you hadn't a care in the world. "Got no secrets, I'm not you."

He smiled but it never reached his eyes. "No, you're not."

"Terry, stop with the bullshit. Whatever we're doing, let's get to it."

McCann passed the folder to you and seeing it like that, closed but accusatory, scared you worse than anything McCann said. Hands shaking, you opened the folder to sheet after sheet staring up at you, and you wanted to vomit. How did he have this stuff? How did anyone have this?

VPNs, burner email accounts...how does he have this?

"Thin cases gone fat. Lots and lots of new evidence...all after you've made your arrests. How's that work, I always wondered. If you'd done it once, maybe even twice, I probably wouldn't have noticed. But, dude, case after case after case?"

"That's how it works," you said.

Tell him, Shannon said. *All those men were guilty. They weren't innocent. They were predators. They were guilty, damnit.*

They needed to be more guilty, you thought.

They were guilty, she said again.

Men like the man who killed Shannon.

"Took me a while to figure it out." McCann leaned back his hands, behind his head. "Had to talk to a bunch of computer guys, but they explained it to me. Actually pretty easy. Send some of the kiddie porn you have on your undercover computer from other cases. Fire up a VPN, use a throwaway email account, send kiddie pix. Then you, Mr. Internet Sex Investigator, finds it during the follow up and boom, bigger, better charges."

The air in his office suddenly tasted foul, like it had gone bad in the time you'd sat there. You swallowed around it and brushed dirt off your pants. "Sounds like a great idea, I wish I'd thought of it. Make guilty men even more guilty? Great idea. Problem is...I never did that. So whatever you think you have, be careful, because you don't actually have squat."

Terry touched the pages between the two of you. "I have this."

"Yeah, curious. My undercover computer doesn't have anything like that on it and I have that computer audited every six months, as you well know, since you get the reports. And if it's from my personal computer at home, then the question would be how you had access. Search warrant? No, 'cause you'd have to provide me with a copy. So you must have broken in and done it on the sly. Hmmm...wonder how legal that is."

This time, Terry laughed. "A little paranoid about what I might find?"

"Fuck you," you said. "This is all crap. You're so convinced I'm jealous of your promotion but...news alert...I couldn't care less about your career track."

"That's bullshit and—"

"The hell it is. You're so pissed off about having to suck your brother's tit and eat his shit that you're looking for someone else to hit. He hits you so you want to hit me. Trouble is, you're making wild guesses and so your swings are worthless. You're not hitting anything."

You expected, hoped for, some sort of reaction, something to put him off balance and back on his heels. He gave you none. Instead, he just nodded. Eventually, he said, "I'm going to tear the Frances J. Hudson case apart and it's going to get me every other case you've ever handled. Every arrest you've ever made. Every case you've ever even watched as the backup officer."

You leaned back in the chair and nodded absently. Yeah, you made guilty men guiltier so no one walked away like they did after Shannon's death, but you did nothing on Frances J. Hudson. Daddy Commander was his own thing, his own nightmare of perverse sexual need and willingness. Terry could look all he wanted, talk to as many computer people as he wanted, do forensics as deep and broad as he could possibly imagine, and you didn't care. You had made some maybe mistakes in your career, maybe cutting corners a little or making a misstep or two, but you did it to keep children safe. And Frances J. Hudson wasn't going to point the way to any of those missteps.

"I'm going to tear you down," McCann said. "You'll be fired, charged, convicted, and spend the rest of your life with the scum you've arrested. Or..."

As much as you hated doing it, you took this bait. "Or?"

"Drop Hudson. I'm going to be Deputy Chief someday, soon, and then Chief. This can all go away and you can keep moving up the ladder, maybe even get your bars."

"I don't want your fucking bars."

McCann shrugged. "Whatevs. You can keep moving up the ladder or I will bring this down on you so fast...you'll think the fucking Hindenburg fell outta the damned sky. It'll burn you alive."

You stood and paced the watch commander's office, your head full of screaming noise. "So all the bad things you think I've done, you're willing to turn the other way if I let this guy go." You eyed him. "Who is this guy?"

"Frances J. Hudson," he said.

"And?"

"Frances Jonathon Hudson."

Mother fucker, you thought, angry that Lieutenant Terry McCann, your old shift mate and maybe once your friend, had to lead you; dot to dot to dot drawing the connective lines for you. *Mother son of a bitching fucker.*

"Frances Jonathon Hudson is my brother."

The titty McCann's been sucking for so long.

Then—Last Thursday, 7:14 a.m.

"Now," you said to Tom. "Right now. Gotta do it now."

"Well, good morning." Tom looked at the papers in your hand. "The search warrant? What's going on?"

"Gotta do it now, Tom. Trust me."

He stared at you, confusion ripe on his face. "I do, never doubt that, but why so fast? You just got the returns on the service provider yesterday. Take a breath, man."

You eyed Tom hard. "Dude, please. Just trust me. If we wait we might lose everything. We gotta get his electronics right now. Right now."

For nearly a half a minute, Tom stared at you. His eyes were hard gray, gunmetal and penetrating. Eventually, he nodded. "Yeah, okay, man, I get you. Listen, Judge Daniels is always in early. He's done a few of these electronics warrants. Shouldn't be a problem."

"Let's go," you said.

While you waited in the judge's outer office, you called your Deputy Chief. He was in charge of the SRT; the "Hut-Hut Boys," your ex-wife called them. "We have to go now. I'm about to get the warrant. We have to go now or we'll never get him."

"Hudson?" he asked.

"Yeah. Right now. Chief, you gotta trust me."

"I do but if I'm calling everyone out to execute a warrant, I need to know why."

You took a deep breath. "Hudson is related."

"Huh?"

"Related to an officer."

Tom shook his head. "Damnit."

"Shit," your Deputy Chief said.

"One of *our* officers. One of our commanding officers."

"Muuhh…thur…*fuck*er."

Now—Sunday 3:47 a.m.

You run at him hard, surprising him. Catch him in the jaw with the barrel of the Kimber. Blood spurts from his mouth, maybe a broken tooth or split gum. He yelps, drops his gun, and stumbles backward but he was a street cop once, he knows how to recover quickly.

He's up on his feet and swinging wildly at you before the blood has made it to the bottom of his chin. He's also gone silent, like you've seen him do in barfight after barfight. Diabetes or not, beer belly or not, years since he's been in a barfight or even a tussle or not, his fists remember steel. They pound like a jackhammer, left/right…left/right. Your jaw and your eyes, even your ears, rock in white-hot pain, like an icepick superheated, jammed straight into your brain.

You fall back, yelping like a schoolboy, and he follows you down, crushing you between himself and the ground. His fists pump, pistons redlining. He catches you between his legs and squeezes, trying to keep his prey still and easily beaten.

You twist, trying to get away from him. He squeezes his knees tighter, keeping you pinned, keeping you from breathing. Your hands come up but he hits so hard, each smack like a small earthquake banging through your entire body. You hear a bone snap, somewhere but are so full of pain you don't know where the break is.

His brother, HardBoppinDaddy, is dead.

You ran the search warrant last Thursday, late at night. It was the quickest you could get the forensics guys, the SRT guys, and everything else you needed together. So as 10:00 p.m. rolled around, you executed the search warrant.

And found nothing.

You arrested Hudson anyway, based on the emails and text messages. The judge gave him light bail, he posted and disappeared and then, late last night, as Saturday crawled into Sunday, you got a call from your deputy chief.

"He's dead. Your case is over."

You wilted in disbelief. HardBoppinDaddy was dead of a self-inflicted gunshot wound to the head.

McCann stops punching for a split second. "You did this, motherfucker."

"No."

He raises a knee, "*You*," jams it into your chest.

Your air is gone now. Like a hand has tightened around you. Is this how a heart attack feels? You'd wondered if you'd hear the bullet but there won't be a bullet. In this shitty street, dank with fetid water and rain, slimy with food and blood and who the fuck knew what else, he was going to asphyxiate you to death.

"He was my brother," Terry says. "He was—"

Your paycheck, you want to say. McCann hated his brother, hated that he had to beg him for money. When you were on shift together, he bitched about it all the time. He hated what his life had become in the face of how Frances J. Hudson's life had blossomed.

A reporter had been on HardBoppinDaddy's front porch when he got home after posting bail, story in hand, first shades of it already online. Hudson had yelled at him, denied everything, and then gone inside and shot himself in the head.

Terry hesitates, slows, his face lost in you don't even give a fuck what. You take advantage, spin hard to the left while grabbing his right hand and hauling it beneath your neck and upper chest. He falls tight down on you and you headbutt him backward, hear his nose crack.

He howls and rolls off you. You scramble up, grab the Kimber, and jam it in his face, hard against his broken nose. "Who are the other girls?"

You hadn't wanted the case to be over, but the suicide ended it. There were other victims out there, young girls HardBoppin-

Daddy had lured, had raped and tied up, whose pictures he had smeared all over the internet. Your computer forensics guy had found nothing on his phone or his tablet or his laptop but had told you those devices had been synched to at least one other device. That device, he'd said, was probably where the pictures and videos were. These devices, he'd said, only had file remnants.

"The fuck should I know?" Terry turns his head, spits, blood and angry saliva. It skirts along the surface of the road, doesn't come near you.

"Where is the other phone...or whatever it is?"

"Fuck you." He laughs. "You tell Tom everything?"

"Tom and command. They all know everything. They know you ordered me to shut it down."

"Didn't tell them about your evidentiary bullshit, though, did you?" McCann snorted blood. "Adding on to the cases. What the fuck were you thinking? You had them, there was no reason to pile on."

"Where is the other device?"

"What the fuck does it matter?" Terry screams. He squares up and you think he wants to go again. "Jon is dead. The case is dead. We're—" His hand moves back and forth between you, bringing both of you into the circle. "We're done. We're finished."

"You, maybe. Not me. I've got more yet."

McCann laughs. "Over for you, bitch. Command knows your dirty little secret."

Fear and rage, a taco truck combination plate that's too hot to eat, fills you. You jam the gun against his face again, pushing him back hard until he trips and hits the ground. "You don't know shit, you asshole. You don't know my secrets."

You thumb the Kimber's hammer back and wrap your finger around the trigger.

Are you ready, Shannon asks. *Are you?*

Yeah, you think, *you are ready.*

"Plural?" Terry asks. "Secrets...plural? What all you got out there, boy?"

You grin and realize your breath is slow and stable, your heart isn't beating its way out of your chest. Maybe you'd wanted to tell someone? Maybe you'd wanted to put the knowledge on someone else's shoulder after all these years? "Shannon's killer."

Confusion stitches across McCann's face. "What? Who's killer?"

"He didn't go to trial. There wasn't enough evidence."

Terry grins. "Ah...Shannon. The great lost love. Raped and killed and no one ever paid for it."

"Oh, but he did," you say.

There is silence for a few seconds. McCann nods when he finally gets it. "Secrets. No statute on that murder."

"Or this one."

When you shoot, it's not at all like killing Shannon's guy. That was in the heat of the moment, the passion of anger and regret and young love.

Still anger and regret, you think. *But cold as shit this time.*

When Lieutenant Terry McCann is dead, three bullets deep and your secrets buried in his blood, you grab his gun, drop the Kimber in the mess, and walk away.

Four Days from Now

You type quickly, relishing the tingle in your belly. You always get it when you start a new project.

Oh, Daddy, you write. *Shannon is so naughty. She needs a strong hand.*

You erase it. Sounds too grown up. After all, you have to convince this guy—Playful Penguin—that you're only thirteen years old.

Don't worry, Shannon says. *You'll get it. You always do.*

Your Deputy Chief slips his head in your office. "Snap it up, we gotta head out to make the funeral."

"Coming. Listen, Chief, we gotta take your car. Mine's dead."

He chuckles. "I told you not to buy crap. Hard metal from Detroit, that's what you want. Get some trade out of it?"

"Hell, no. When I say dead, I mean dead. Undercarriage rotted out."

"All the damned road salt the county uses."

"Yeah, well, whatever it was, it dropped damn near in the middle of the road. I just scrapped it. Got a few bucks." The truth is you managed to drive it to Baraboo, Wisconsin, to a friend's scrapyard. He laughed about you using it for target practice while each of you put another few hundred rounds through it, better a beer per shot. Then he crushed it while you watched. Easy-peasy, no sweat or fuss.

McCann's gun is in the Des Plains river and Ashlee's sister, a trauma nurse in East St. Louis, came up for a few days to quietly tend the through-and-through bullet hole in your shoulder. She isn't totally convinced by Ashlee's story of you dropping your duty Glock, getting a shoulder shot in return, and being too embarrassed to let anyone at the PD know what a fucktard you were. Not totally convinced, you can see it in her eyes, but she's comfortable after grilling Ashlee repeatedly about domestic violence.

"Gotta take care of that shoulder," the chief says as you wince. "Torn muscles can be hell. Stay off the weight, weak sister. You can go to the funeral, right?"

"Absolutely. We were partners once. I'm going."

The chief's face tightens. "Always assumed I'd attend Terry's funeral...just didn't think it'd be this way."

"Any leads?"

"Other than the Kimber that killed him? Fuck no. Nothing anywhere. On his phones or computer. His email is empty. No fucking idea what he was doing out there."

You almost toss Terry on his half-brother's pile of ash. It'd be easy to do. But you don't, no idea why.

Your DC snaps his fingers. "Let's go."

"Yeah, gimme a second. Lemme finish this email."

"A new project?"

You nod, bang out something quick, attach one of the pictures, and hit Send.

Good boy, Shannon says.

GUNS + TACOS · CREATED AND EDITED BY   MICHAEL BRACKEN & TREY R. BARKER

WILLIAM DYLAN POWELL

SOME CHURROS AND EL BURRO

SEASON 1

GUNS + TACOS

EPISODE 5

BOOKS BY WILLIAM DYLAN POWELL

*Untimely Demise: A Darkly Humorous Presentation
of 365 Deadly Deeds*

Non-Fiction
100 Things to Do in Houston Before You Die
Austin Then & Now
Houston Then & Now
Lost Houston
*Secret Houston: A Guide to the Weird, Wonderful,
and Obscure*
Texas Then & Now

SOME CHURROS AND EL BURRO

William Dylan Powell

Just East of Cosala, Sinaloa, Mexico

Chispa sat in his rusty Chevy Lumina, draining the last of his *horchata*. An open copy of *Empires of Light* sat in his lap, the sweat from his hair dripping on the pages. He'd pulled into the gate five minutes ago and knew the guards were watching him; probably people inside the *palacio* too. Maybe even Dante Garcia himself. But he couldn't help procrastinating. It was like the very idea of entering the place where Dante Garcia slept was being rejected by his brain. Eventually, though, he could delay no more.

The door squeaked like a coffin as Chispa opened it and stepped out. As he approached the house, a small jet took to the sky from Dante Garcia's private runway, and Chispa badly wished he were onboard. Wherever it was going. The door opened before he could knock. Dante's lieutenant, Alejandro, looked harried.

"What were you doing out there, *Chispa*? Come on. He's getting *loco* in there."

Why did El Patrón ask me to help Dante Garcia? Chispa thought. *Of all people it had to be Dante Garcia. It couldn't be old lady Vargas, or El Scorpion's brother, who lets me play Red Dead Redemption II on the PS4. It had to be Dante Garcia.*

A few years ago, Tomas "Chispa" Busch was just another foot soldier for the Sangre Cartel. Orphaned. A dropout at age fourteen. He did what he had to for survival. But bored standing lookout at a police station one day, he fixed a diamond-encrusted iPhone X *Los Payaso* had dropped during a shootout at Las Tetas Sports Bar & Grill in Mazatlan. Shortly thereafter, he rewired El Pastor's Ford Raptor to play *De Sinaloa Para El Mundo* by Calibre 50 whenever the alarm remote was pressed. Then he installed a surveillance center and media server at Antonio *El Demonio*'s house, mostly so *El Demonio* would know where his wife was at all times. Finding a real passion for the work, he spent the rest of his childhood doing his best to educate himself in all things electrical.

Soon people came to him for all kinds of electronics and computer work, dubbing him *la chispa*, "the spark."

Chispa followed Alejandro between the giant brass lions at the front door, through the home's gilded center hallway, beneath its outsized family portraits and paintings of matadors, and to a spacious office at the back of the house.

On one wall hung a large, curved screen with a video feed featuring a man wearing blue overalls at an auto shop. Outside the shop's door, a foot of snow stood on the ground. The man looked cold and scared. Dante Garcia was screaming at him through the computer.

"Your spreadsheet is *jodido*, *pendejo*. You think I don't have people all over Chicago lined up to replace you? This ain't MetLife, motherfucker. This ain't *All Things Considered*. I will cut off everything, sew it all back where it don't belong and send you to the bottom of the lake in a god-damned barrel."

"Calm down, Jefe. It's not that bad..." The face on the screen froze, the man's mouth an awkward shape. One gold tooth caught the light from a nearby welder.

"You see?" Dante Garcia turned to Chispa. "This is why I call. Seven thousand on this *maldito* laptop, all the best cameras, the best satellite internet. This choppy, broken *mierda* is what I get."

"Okay, Señor Garcia," said Chispa, poking at some computer keys and wiggling some wires, "Let me see what I can do."

As Chispa poked around, the frozen face on the screen came back to life.

"Can you hear me?" said the man on the screen.

"I don't think so," said Dante Garcia, pulling a nickel-plated .357 revolver from his waistband and spinning the chamber. "It sounded like you were just telling me I don't know how to read a spreadsheet. Or that I'm some stupid *hijo de puta* who likes giving money away. But that's not what you were saying. Right?"

The man on the screen widened his eyes. "What? No. Don Garcia, no, I was just saying the numbers are pretty flat except for alternators. I admit, we didn't sell hardly any alternators now three months."

"And why is that? I spent three years freezing my *culo* off in Chicago. There's, like, fifty colleges. Plus all those young lawyers and artists and shit. You can't tell me nobody wants... alternators."

"I've got Big..." The man's face froze again, his arms gesturing out wide. The audio looped, repeating "big, big, big, big..."

"Chispa!" screamed Dante, "Fix this fucking thing. What am I paying you for?"

Chispa checked a few more things, then looked up. "I don't see any problem with your computer. I need to go troubleshoot the hardware." Then he ran from the room as if it were on fire. Alejandro had disappeared completely.

"Can you hear me now?" asked the face on the screen.

"Yes, for the love of Jesus Malverde, I can hear you."

"Anyway," said the man on the screen, "there's someone else selling alternators up here. A new brand. 'Route 66.' Nobody wants just plain old ecstasy anymore."

"Alternators."

"Yes, alternators. Right. Nobody wants the normal stuff now. But, I mean, it's just alternators. We make so much on everything else..."

The two talked about all the other types of parts they sold in the area—engines and transmissions and other euphemisms for their products that go in through Texas and up I-35 to make up the bulk of the Sangre Cartel's annual revenue. The truth was, Garcia's Chicago distributorship made so much money on meth, coke, heroin, and weed that the ecstasy sales were equivalent to a rounding error. But Dante Garcia didn't like sharing, just on principle.

They were about to wrap up the call when Dante asked: "So who is it?"

"*Quién es quién?*" said the man on the screen.

"Who's captured the 'alternator' market up there?"

"Oh, just some college kid. It's pretty *chido*, actually. A little red Corvette with a Route 66 sign on a piece of paper. Dissolves in water and tastes like bitter cherries. Usually *éxtasis* is just a pill. I did some while banging this Dominican over in Skokie."

"TMI, *'mano*, Jesus. Nobody down here wants to hear about your whores."

"Makes your hair feel funny, you know? Even, like, your arm hairs."

"Seriously, *'mano*, shut the fuck up."

"Anyway, I sent Big Winkie to talk to the kid. We'll get it back soon. I've got piles of *éxtasi*...er...alternators up here in storage. I'm still bringing it in, but it's starting to stack up like *pinche* Beanie Babies from the nineties."

The image froze again, the man in the middle of wiping his nose on his sleeve.

All traces of emotion faded from Dante Garcia's face. He flicked the chamber closed on the revolver.

It was the worst possible time for Chispa to walk back into the room.

"Bad news," said Chispa. "Your computer, the camera, the satellite system, everything checks out. So, the problem is the airstrip. Has to be."

"What do you mean?"

"Well, radar can cause satellite interference, so I think that's your problem. It's the only thing that makes sense."

"Just fix it, you fucking *empollón*. Now."

"Okay," said Chispa. "Actually, that's what I mean. There is no real fix for this unless you refrain from using the radar from the airstrip, or from all aircraft, when you want to use the internet. Either that or transition to a fiber-optic internet or something. We're pretty far out of town, so I'm not sure what the infrastructure is like. *Lo siento*, Señor Garcia."

"So, you're saying you can't fix it?"

The man on the screen came back to life. "Can you hear me Señor Garcia? Hooollllaaaaa..."

Dante Garcia raised the revolver and emptied it into the flat screen.

The noise deafened Chispa. He ducked as black plastic flew everywhere and the room filled with the smell of shots fired.

"Well?" asked Dante Garcia. "Are any solutions suddenly coming to mind?"

Chispa stood, ears ringing. "I'm sorry, Jefe. I want to help, but it's not a go-fix-it kind of problem. It's just an inherent conflict in these systems."

"Oh," said Dante Garcia. "Inherent conflict." He set the revolver back on his desk, a thin tendril of smoke still rising from the weapon.

"You're that *Germano-Mexicano* from Palenque, right? The orphan from *El Phantasma*'s crew?"

Chispa nodded.

"You like fixing things?"

"Sí," said Chispa. "I very much like fixing things."

"Good. Good. That's good. Well you see, I like breaking things. I very much like breaking things. You could say it's the only thing I've ever been any good at." His face broke into an enormous smile. "Be out front at 4 a.m. tomorrow morning. Not a minute later."

"*Que?*" asked Chispa. "Why? I told Don Lopez I would help him with that journalist over in Los Mochis, then run conduit for his new garage."

"Fuck Lopez," said Dante Garcia. "And fuck that journalist too. You think you're so smart, you can go to Chicago instead. You're going to help fix my alternator problem."

Chicago, Illinois

Tucker Mitchell and his friends stumbled out of The Crooked Bat at 2:13 p.m. that same day to find Big Winkie smoking a cigarette and leaning against Tuck's prized Dodge Hellcat. Tucker shouldn't even have driven the thing that day, what with the steady snow and the car's ludicrous racing slicks. But they always went to The Crooked Bat during football season and today was Penny Pitchers. Plus, it was a sweet ass ride.

"Excuse me," Tucker said, jingling his keys and staring at the man. "We're taking off over here. *S'il vous plaît laissez,* my good man."

Oversized and sporting neck tats, the hulking man had the look of a former NFL player who'd let himself go and was angry at the world. The world in general, but Tucker Mitchell in particular.

Tucker's best friend and fraternity brother, Chad Lewis, was with him—along with a skinny pledge named Flip.

Big Winkie squinted and flicked his cigarette at Tucker's loafers.

"Hey! Watch it, man. What's your problem?"

"You Tucker Mitchell, right? The little shit that's been sellin' X to anyone with a pulse?"

Tucker froze. In his mind, he saw a swarm of DEA agents leaping from the bushes to ruin his life forever. Shitty jail food. Poor people germs. Worse things. But the street was quiet. Just some girls window shopping and a young couple across the street building a snowman on the trunk of a Volvo.

"Who the hell are you?" asked Tucker, crossing his arms.

The big man stood up straight, the car rising in relief.

"I'm the motherfucker that was sent to let you know you're out of business. For good."

"What?" Tucker said, with a haughty chuckle. "You can't

talk to me like that. Do you know who I am?"

"Kick his ass, Tuck," said Chad, taking off his Ray Bans.

Flip the pledge dipped into his duffle and came out with a lacrosse stick.

"Yeah, Tuck," said Big Winkie, taking a step toward Tucker. "Kick his ass."

The window-shopping girls stopped, sensing a fight brewing. Each began recording on their phones.

"Hang on a second," said Tucker, stepping back. "Who are you again? Is he with you?"

Tucker pointed over Big Winkie's shoulder. When Winkie turned his head, Tucker put everything he had into a right cross. The punch landed with a wet, smacking sound. Tucker flexed his hand over and over, sure something had broken inside.

Big Winkie rocked back with the blow and raised his eyebrows, placing a hand on the Hellcat for balance. Then he smiled.

Flip dropped the lacrosse stick.

"Dude. I was just kidding." said Tucker. "Can't you take a joke?"

Big Winkie grabbed the front of Tucker's Nantucket red plaid blazer and hoisted him a foot-and-a-half above the ground. The girls holding the phones never said a single word during the entire altercation. Not "stop" or "help" or "somebody call 911." But they finally broke their silence when the dark spot spread down Tuck's Banana Republic chinos. They broke their silence by giggling. One of them said: "Oh my Godddddddd…"

Chispa awoke when Chorro slammed on the brakes. His copy of *The Art of Electronics* slid onto the floorboard of the beat up Suburu, along with the dregs of his gas station coffee.

"*Baboso,*" said Chorro, swerving around a school bus. "Rock and roll, rock and roll, c'mon, motherfuckers." Chorro's leg pumped up and down, his eyes wide and round as shotgun slugs. He punched the steering wheel and held his fist on the horn.

For Chispa, the trip had been torture. Dante Garcia had arranged a ride to Chicago with a drug mule who was being paid $300, and a 1992 Subaru SVX with one primer fender, to smuggle a few bricks of special-order heroin hidden in the car. And hidden in Chorro himself.

The border crossing went well, but by the time they reached Fort Worth Chispa had agreed to give Chorro another $300 to be quiet so he could just read the rest of the trip. Dante Garcia had fronted Chispa a few thousand dollars as a per diem, and Chispa figured he'd just eat a little less. It was something he'd gotten good at after his parents had died.

But Chorro had scored some speed in East St. Louis to stay awake during the last of the thirty-four-hour drive, and then chattered like a nervous gameshow contestant the whole way up Interstate 55.

Chispa yawned and wiped coffee from his book onto the floorboard.

"Careful with that, *empollón*," said Chorro without taking his eyes off the road. "This is my ride now, and I don't want coffee and shit everywhere."

The Suburu looked like it had seen service in Afghanistan, but Chispa apologized and checked his watch.

The land was flat, with a lot of open space and scrubby grass. They passed by a huge refinery, went over a sturdy metal bridge, and past signs reading "Historic Route 66" and "Morris" and "Joliet." It wasn't until they were in the city proper the place even vaguely resembled the Chicago he'd seen in *The Blues Brothers* movie shown at the *orfanato*.

When Chorro said they were going to a place called Riverdale, Chispa envisioned an office of glass and steel surrounded by green hills and clear water. But Riverdale's Consolidated Auto Care was a rusted-out warehouse between a water treatment plant and the kind of public housing high-rise Chispa had only seen in American rap videos. Out front, three shabby men passed a liquor bottle between them as they gathered around a metal barrel with a fire burning inside.

Fosforo, the gold-toothed man he'd seen on Dante Garcia's video screen, came to meet them as they pulled up.

"Hey, *'manos*," Fosforo said, slapping the hood of the car and holding up a bottle of Buchanan's scotch.

Chispa collected his things, opened the door and stepped out. He had to lean on the roof before trusting his legs to support his weight after the grueling drive, and the cold made his whole body feel like he'd fallen into a cactus.

Chorro and Fosforo shook and exchanged a few words, the steam from their breath lingering. Chispa joined them in front of the body shop, limping a little with one leg asleep.

"You *mariconitos* ready to party?" said Fosforo. "I got *yayo*, I got bitches, I got everything. And you ain't payin' for jack shit yo. Tonight, it's on me."

Chorro smiled. "Yeaaah, boy. That's what I'm talkin' about. I been stuck smelling this *empollón*'s farts for days. It's been like church. I'm ready to get fucked up, yo."

Chispa pulled out the iPhone Dante Garcia had given him, studying a map of the area and ordering a ride. He didn't know Chicago. He'd never even been to Mexico City. But he knew he still had plenty of per diem for now and wasn't going to waste a night in America getting into trouble with Chorro and Fosforo. "That sounds sweet," said Chispa. "But I've got work to do, *'manos*. For Don Garcia."

"See?" said Chorro. "This is what I'm talking about."

"What's the matter?" asked Fosforo. "You don't want to hang out? I promised Dante Garcia I would show you a good time. Don't make a liar of me. Big Winkie's already talked to this college kid." Fosforo looked scared now, and a little hurt. Chispa recalled the tense video conference.

"No, Don Fosforo, it's not that," said Chispa. "*Lo ciento*, it sounds *chido*, really. But you know how Dante Garcia is. I want to take care of business first, then come back and party with you guys. I just want to do a good job for him. Don't you?"

Fosforo snapped his fingers and smiled, his gold tooth glinting in the sunset. "A man of business. I respect that." Fosforo took an envelope out of the pocket of his greasy blue overalls and handed it to Chispa.

"Here's everything on the guy you're looking for. He's just a stupid *escuincle*. I mean, he's probably about your age. What are you, twenty?"

"*Diecinueve*," said Chispa.

"I'm just saying, you'll have plenty of time to party with us when you're done."

"Okay, *suena bien*," said Chispa. "*Gracias*."

The Uber driver pulled up, looking fidgety. Chispa got inside.

"Tony Hotel Hyde Park?" asked the driver.

"Yes," said Chispa. He'd picked a random hotel closer to the lake and the city proper. He didn't know anything about the place, but it had to be better than sharing a back room at Consolidated Auto Care. As the driver pulled away, heater on full blast, Chispa opened his copy of *The Art of Electronics* and read in silence. The hotel was already worth the money.

"I should have just kicked his ass then and there," said Tucker. "But I was holding back."

"You didn't hold much back," said Flip, snickering.

"Fuck you, pledge," said Chad. "Keep talking shit and see what happens."

Flip rolled his eyes but didn't push his luck.

"Where'd you hear about this 'Jesse' lady?" Chad asked Tucker.

Tucker kept his eyes on the road and said nothing.

"Tuck," said Chad. "You okay?"

Tucker Mitchell was still going over what happened in his head, trying to come to terms with it. Make sense of it.

He'd ducked into a nearby coffee shop earlier and put on a pair of golfing shorts he kept in the car—stuffing the offending chinos in the coffee shop's trashcan. In all his time making and selling Route 66, this was the first time he'd ever actually encountered a criminal. An actual criminal. Sure, making and selling ecstasy was illegal but Tucker didn't consider himself a real criminal. Not really.

"I'm sorry," said Tucker. "What did you say, man?"

"I asked how come you knew about this taco truck."

"Oh, yeah. So, I went to Lake Forest with this kid who transferred out because his family went bust," Tuck said. "I mean, they fell *hard*. He ended up in some South Side shithole. His first day at school some guys stole his shoes. Someone felt sorry for him and told him about this food truck. Later he told me. Apparently, you just roll up and order. They give you the food, and a gun. You have to just take whatever they give you."

"That sounds sketchy," said Flip.

"Of course, it's sketchy," said Tucker. "It's sketchy as fuck. But I'm not having that happen again. Ever."

"What happened to your friend?" asked Chad.

"Who?"

"The guy whose family went broke."

"Oh, he wasn't really my friend, just some guy. Basically, his life was ruined. He got his ass kicked every day and ended up studying law at some state school. But he was always a loser."

In one thousand feet, said the car's navigation system, *turn right.*

"Jesus, look at this place," said Flip. "It's like *Road Warrior*."

They were in Fuller Park on a residential street composed of short, squat beige- and brick-colored homes with weedy yards and cement front steps. A group of young men stopped their basketball game when they saw the bright-red Hellcat pull onto the lane. Despite the cold, most of the boys wore thin gray hoodies and long basketball shorts.

Tucker locked the doors. "It moves around, so we'll have to

find it first or we're not getting shit." They stopped at a stop sign with "51st Boyz" spray painted on it and looked both ways. Tucker picked a direction and turned.

After just ten minutes of searching, they finally spotted the taco truck at the end of a barren road. It was parked next to a fenced in junkyard full of old Chicago Police Department patrol cars in various states of decay.

Tucker drove the Hellcat to the end of the street, then turned around—ready for a quick getaway.

"Stay Gold, Pony Boy," said Tucker, putting the car in park and jumping out. His legs were freezing, the golf shorts not doing much by way of winter warmth. As he approached the food truck, the smell of it hit him like a pledge paddle to the face: a combination of weed, onions and feet. He felt queasy.

"Good morning," said Tucker, walking up to the truck. "I'm looking for Jessie."

"I'm Jesse," said the man at the window—a stocky Asian guy with tat sleeves and a ponytail. He was reading a *hentai* comic featuring a ridiculously voluptuous woman doing unspeakable things with a tentacled alien.

"Wait," said Tucker. "What? I thought Jesse was a woman."

"What are you trying to say?" said the man, setting down his comic book and glaring.

Inside the truck a dwarf cooking an unidentifiable meat on the grill smirked, his cigarette jutting off at a funny angle.

"What? No. Oh, no, sir. It's just I was confused."

The man leaned out of the window and squinted at Tucker. "You hungry or not?"

"Oh, uh. Right. Let's see." Tucker looked at the stained menu on the side of the truck. Item by item he tried to decipher if his food order would determine what kind of gun he'd get.

"They look like sweet little boys," said the dwarf at the grill. "I think they want some nice churros."

"You want some churros?" said the man at the window.

"Uh, yeah. Sure. Churros." Tucker didn't know what a churro

was, but he knew he would certainly never actually ingest anything that came from this rolling bacteria farm.

The dwarf reached into a small fridge and came out with some rolled up dough, already covered in sugar and cinnamon, then plopped it into some grease.

"Two-fifty," said Jesse.

"Right," said Tucker, glancing around nervously as he took out his wallet. He removed three hundred-dollar bills and handed them over. Jesse took the money and stuck it in his apron, then went back to his comic book. The dwarf took the churros out of the grease and dried them—finally throwing them into a brown paper bag with something shiny.

"So, I guess just keep the change," said Tucker as he took the bag. Jesse never looked up from his comic as Tuck got back into the Hellcat and sped off, asking the car's navigation system for the fastest route possible back to the Tau Theta Alpha house.

The next morning, Chispa had a quiet breakfast at the Tony Hyde Park Hotel. He'd taken a shower and slept for almost twelve hours. He couldn't remember ever getting that much sleep or sleeping in such luxury. At breakfast he read from *Empires of Light* as a girl about his age in a sleek, black suit refilled his coffee.

"You a Burgundy?" she asked.

"*Que?*"

"A student?" She pointed at his book.

"Oh, yes," he said. "Engineering." He startled himself with the ease of the lie.

"You look the type," she said, placing the bill for his pancakes on the table with a smile. "The south side of Chicago. Where fun goes to die. Isn't that what all you smart kids say?"

After breakfast, Chispa decided on a walk. The cold no longer felt so terrible after a night's sleep, pancakes and coffee. Soon he saw why the waitress had confused him with a student. His hotel was by a huge university.

Despite the ruthless cold, people all around him rode bikes through streets lined with neatly kept houses and buildings of steel and glass; brick and ivy; old, arched designs like the Catholic churches back home. Young men and women his age walked in clumps between buildings and huddled together at tables in coffee shops. There was an energy to the place Chispa had a hard time articulating to himself. Like everyone was getting ready for something big; like having so many focused people in one place changed the air.

Chispa ducked into a bookstore, spending almost two hours browsing books on physics, electrical engineering, electromagnetics and nanotechnology. On his way out, he picked up a course catalog.

Back at the TTA house, Tucker parked the Hellcat and marched straight upstairs without talking to anyone. He threw the churros, which smelled like burned hair, into his trash can. Then he brought the gun to his desk, turning on a lamp to study it.

It was easily the tackiest gun he'd ever seen. A gold-plated Colt 1911 with an engraving of a donkey's head on the grip and the words "*El Burro*" etched on the barrel. There was a diamond embedded into one of the donkey's teeth.

"Jesus H. Christ," he whispered to himself. "That is some ridiculous bullshit." He plucked a few boxes of Kleenex from a box on his desk and did his best to remove the grease from the churros.

Tucker jumped when the knock came at the door. He shoved *El Burro* into his desk just as Bryce Graham walked in.

"Tuuuuuuuuck," said Bryce shaking hands with Tucker. "You okay, man?"

Tucker wiped sweat from his forehead and ran a hand through his feathery blond hair. "Of course. What's up?"

Bryce flipped a nearby chair backwards and straddled it,

then let out a deep breath. He looked serious. "Dude, I wanted to talk privately because I've got an ask for you and it's a big one. It's also not negotiable. And I'm hoping we can work it out because I have a lot of respect for you. Even if you did go to Lake Forest."

Tucker gave Bryce the finger.

"All kidding aside, you being third generation TTA in this chapter really carries a lot of weight. The support your family gives. That fucking gaming pod you donated, which is sick as shit by the way."

Tucker crossed his arms, waiting for the "but."

Bryce reached into his shirt pocket and set a tiny plastic bag on the table, approximately the size of a postage stamp. Inside was a red and white decal of a corvette and racing flags with Route 66 at the top. "But this is the last time we're going to have this conversation," said Bryce. "Either you quit with this bullshit or you're out. And if you think I'm bluffing, just try me."

The bright red Hellcat caught Birgit Olson's eye when it appeared in front of Roasters Coffee. She was polishing up a paper on American Cultural Metaphors in Color Theory, so the sight of the cherry red muscle car against the white snow made an impact.

Birgit only knew two people in Chicago: Darcy, the hypochondriac roommate she'd been assigned by the school at random, and one of the Mean Girls from her high school back home in Wisconsin, who she took pains to avoid. So, she enjoyed coming to Roasters each afternoon—partly for their chocolate macarons but also just to be around people.

As a young man stepped from the car into the coffee shop, Birgit continued studying his colors: The flaxen hair sticking up every which way. The red, plaid blazer. The pale complexion. The kid ordered a latte and sat at the table next to hers, leaning his head back and closing his eyes.

"Rough morning?" she asked.

He opened one eye and looked at her. "Dude, you have no idea."

She smiled. "Haven't seen you here before."

"Nobody has. That's why I'm here. I'm, like, hiding in plain sight or something."

"Yeah," said Birgit. "I kind of do that every day." They spent the next hour talking. She talked about her hometown in Wisconsin, her graphic design studies and the roommate who claimed to have eosinophilic pneumonia. He talked about his plans to be a big shot investment banker and move to New York or London or Shanghai.

Birgit could tell he wasn't that bright. And he did hold much of the conversation staring at her chest. But he was certainly handsome. And if she was being honest with herself, it had been a long time since she'd talked to anyone other than Dying Darcy. So, when he asked her to attend the Aliens and Astronauts party at the Tau Theta Alpha house that night, she agreed without hesitation.

"What do you mean he's not there?" Dante Garcia asked Fosforo on the big screen. "Chorro made his delivery, so I know they got there okay."

"No, it's all good," said Fosforo. He and four topless women were in his auto shop cutting cocaine with SpringFresh laundry detergent. He kept sifting product through a strainer as they talked. "Your man is out tracking the dude down or some shit. Said he had a plan. Didn't even want to party with us last night."

Dante Garcia took the cigar out of his mouth and laughed until he coughed. "No shit he didn't want to party. That guy is a total *endeble*. He's just the computer nerd. *Punto* thinks he so smart. We'll see how smart he feels on the streets." Fosforo heard the sound of an airplane in the background come through over the computer speaker.

On Fosforo's screen, Dante Garcia's face froze in mid-laughter. A minute later, when the screen unfroze, Dante Garcia held his revolver—pointing it at the camera again.

"Calm down, Jefe," said Fosforo.

"Tell that fucking *empollón* that if he doesn't fix your alternator problem in twenty-four hours, I'll send someone after *him*." Dante Garcia stared straight into the camera and tightened his grip on the gun. The screen went dead.

Birgit didn't have a car, and Tucker never offered to come get her—or to have dinner beforehand. She Ubered to the party after receiving a text from him about an hour before: "U still down?" with an alien emoji. Not exactly romance, but still a break from the Photoshop tutorials and episodes of *The Amazing English Baking Contest* which had awaited her otherwise.

She'd found a pair of oversized headphones and some coveralls she'd bought for a painting class, cutting a miniature satellite dish out of a paper plate and painting it. *Et voilà: Jodie Foster in Contact*, she thought. It was all she could muster at the last minute, and she still felt a little uncomfortable about it. Always insecure about her weight, she imagined herself looking like a stuffed potato in the coveralls.

When she arrived at the party, the other girls didn't do much to assuage her insecurities.

"What are you supposed to be?" asked a girl in skin-tight silver with glittery eye makeup.

"Jodie Foster in *Contact*," she said, holding up her cardboard satellite dish and waggling it around.

"Oh," said the Girl From the Future, snickering. "I thought you were ground crew from O'Hare. I was about to yell at you for losing my luggage." The girl burst out laughing, spilling her wine and stumbling away to join a guy with a half-sunburned face in a game of oversized Jenga.

Birgit finally caught up with Tucker in the media room,

where *Cloverfield* was playing on a giant screen.

"It's aliens!" Tucker said, his hands in front of him. He was dressed in a grayish-brown suit and tie; his hair was gelled to stick straight up.

"Oh, that's good," she said, "you're Giorgio Tsoukalos. Clever."

"What? No, girl, I'm Alien Meme Guy. You Know: It's Aliens." Again, he squinted and held his hands out in front of himself.

"Right, yeah. Giorgio Tsoukalos. From Switzerland. Did you know he speaks, like, five languages?"

"You have to see the meme," said Tucker, handing Birgit a red plastic cup. "C'mon, the movie just started."

They watched *Cloverfield* on an overstuffed brown leather loveseat, a pair of pledges named Flip and Lance keeping their cups full.

She noticed the other boys treating Tuck with deference, and though he did lay on the body spray a little thick she enjoyed the warmth of him—his arm wrapping around her about the time the Statue of Liberty's head rolled along the streets of Manhattan. And she got goose bumps when she pretended to punch him jokingly in the stomach and felt the hardness of his stomach beneath his shirt and tie. After that, she'd been distracted by the physical reality of him. She actually hated *Cloverfield*, with all that jostling camerawork and cheesy bro dialogue, but still found herself disappointed when the credits began rolling.

After the movie there was a costume contest in which a pair of green, big-headed aliens who'd hobbled around the party on stilts all night took the prize for Most Awesome Costume in the Universe. After the award was granted, black lights were switched on to reveal glowing stars, moons and planets drawn all over the house. Moby's "We're All Made of Stars" began playing and the place erupted in dance.

Birgit danced for hours. She danced with Tuck, and Tuck's friends, and some of the other girls, and by herself, and she didn't once think about how she really didn't know any of these people, or anyone else in Chicago, or about her exhausting roommate or how she'd soon need a job after graduation. She just let herself be happy and free, dancing and screaming and singing along with the others and drinking from the cup Flip and Lance never let run dry and feeling, for once, less alone.

At some point, Tuck brought her a bottle of water. She guzzled the whole thing, not wanting to be hung over in the morning. It tasted like bitter cherries.

They danced to "Little Fluffy Clouds" by The Orb. After a few minutes, he took off her oversized headphones and ran his hands through her hair.

Goosebumps raced across her scalp and she gasped. It felt incredible, like electricity running through her. He touched her face with his fingertips as they danced, and she shivered with delight. She couldn't remember anything feeling so good. Her heartbeat like a motorcycle engine. She kissed him—at first fumbling and strange but soon finding a rhythm. The sensation was like a warm bath.

She hardly remembered them stumbling upstairs to his room.

"My God, this place is so clean," she said, taking in the room. "I always pictured frat houses as disgusting boy caves."

"The shower's not always pretty," Tuck said. "I'm not gonna lie. Still, though, we have maids and a house mother and, for the really nasty jobs, pledges."

"Ew," she said, holding up one hand and swinging her headphones with the other. "I don't want to hear anything else about fraternity hygiene."

"Speaking of," he said. "Give me a minute." He stumbled off to the bathroom and Birgit sat at the young man's desk. She was tired and drunk and her face felt like the surface of the sun. Her jumpsuit was wet with the sweat of her dancing in the stuffy house with three hundred strangers. She rested her head on the cool, polished wood of his desk. It smelled like lemons.

He seemed to be taking forever.

When the desk started spinning, she sat up and turned on his desk light. To take her mind off the dizziness, she pulled open Tucker's desk drawer.

There was no missing *El Burro*.

"Holy shit," she whispered, picking up the weapon and feeling its heft in her hands. *Was this thing real?* She mashed a button above the trigger, feeling it engage with a metal click. Then she pushed the button back the way it was and hurriedly replaced it, closing the drawer. *El Burro? What in the world is that all about?*

Tuck came in, smiling. "It's Aliens!" he said, his fingers outstretched. The two giggled as he guided her to the bed. She smiled and closed her eyes as they kissed.

The jumpsuit had one long zipper, which Tucker made quick work of. The cool air felt delicious on her skin. He kissed her gently on the cheek, then the chin, then the side of her neck. Then he began working his way down, painstakingly slow.

"Oh, God," she gasped. The heat within her seemed unbearable, and she put her hands to her neck, flicking her long hair out and away from her. A crash came from beside the bed. *My headphones!*

"Oh shit," she said, sitting up. "What did I just break?" Birgit looked bedside to see a picture of herself on a computer screen, braless and shirtless and glassy-eyed. Her *Phasers on Stun* tattoo was plainly visible.

"What the fuck?" she screamed.

"Oh, shit," said Tuck. "It's not what you think."

"What the fuck?" Birgit repeated, pulling a pillow in front of herself and scrambling to find her jumpsuit. "Are you some kind of pervert or something?"

"No," he said. "I swear to God that's just a mistake. I was, like, Skyping or something. Earlier." Tuck switched off the monitor on the bedside computer. From the angle of the video, she could tell that the camera itself was in a nearby closet—the screen's image bracketed between two of the slots in the folding closet door.

Birgit shoved each foot into her damp coveralls as if trying to poke holes in something, tears blurring her vision. "I can't believe you," she said, doing her best to hold back an angry sob.

"I can't believe *you're* making such a big deal about this," Tucker said. "You know, you're lucky I invited someone like you tonight anyway."

"Fuck you," she said, zipping up her jumpsuit and running from the room.

The address Fosforo had given Chispa was within walking distance of Chispa's hotel: A fraternity house. When he arrived, a huge party was in full swing. People came and went from what looked like an enormous mansion—each boy or girl dressed as a UFO, an outlandish space alien, or an astronaut in a space suit. People spilled out into the front yard, driveway, and street; hundreds of people.

During the walk over, Chispa had Googled the concept of Greek life on American college campuses, but still struggled to get his head around the idea. Nevertheless, when he got there it looked like an incredible party. And as he walked across the lawn in his newly purchased South Chicago University sweatshirt, he couldn't help but notice all the girls—exceptionally pretty even when dressed as Russian Cosmonauts or painted green.

Two big men in SCU football jerseys stood at the front door of the TTA house, their hair in identical buzzcuts.

"*Hola*," said Chispa. "I'm looking for Tucker Mitchell, please."

"Pretty sure he's busy," said one of buzzcuts, winking.

"Oh, I'm in his Management of Financial Derivatives class. Exchange student."

"Sorry, bro. Brothers and sisters only tonight. Plus, it's Aliens and Astronauts. You'd be breaking the dress code. Couldn't let you in if I wanted."

"Oh, right. Yes, it looks like a lot of fun." Chispa leaned toward the nearest buzzcut. "You know, technically speaking, I am actually an alien. From Mexico." He smiled.

The buzzcut looked alarmed. "Whoa. Isn't that, like, racist or something? The fraternity doesn't go around, you know, appropriating shit or whatever."

Chispa laughed. "It's just a little joke. Is everyone in America so serious all the time? I only need five minutes, tops. One quick question."

Just then a girl burst from the front door and ran into Chispa like a linebacker. The two both fell onto the hard, frigid sidewalk.

"Hey!" said Chispa, grabbing his elbow. "*Que cojones?*"

The girl's cheeks were flush; she was dressed like a sweaty auto mechanic and holding a painted paper plate. She batted away the buzzcuts, who'd tried to help her up. Then she stood and marched away across the snowy lawn.

"Fuck all of you," she screamed as she walked into the night. "And nobody likes *Cloverfield*, assholes!"

Chispa stood, brushing the snow from his pants.

"Actually," said one of the buzzcuts, "if I'm not mistaken, I'll bet he's free now." He looked at his watch. "You got five minutes," he said, giving Chispa a glow-in-the-dark wristband and nodding toward the door.

Chispa floated around the party for a few minutes, eventually recognizing one of the boys in the kitchen from a picture Fosforo had provided. He was making a tall sandwich from a large tray of bread, meat and cheese.

Chispa's stomach growled involuntarily when he saw the huge table of food, which was largely untouched. He had to remind himself he was there on business.

"Excuse me," said Chispa, extending his hand. "You don't know me, but my name is Tomás Busch. People call me Chispa. Do you have a few minutes to chat? Maybe outside?"

Tucker paused and looked around before shaking the man's hand.

"Something you can't say here?" Tucker set down his rocket ship-themed paper plate, the tower of white bread, ham, Swiss cheese, and pickles collapsing sideways.

Chispa took a mini baggie from his shirt pocket. The tab was broken in half, but the Route 66 was still visible. "It's about your business."

Tucker snatched the baggie from the man. "What is wrong with you?" he hissed, grabbing Chispa by the sweatshirt and leading him away.

Out back, Tucker lit a cigarette—careful never to leave the porch. His eyes darted around the backyard into the shrubs, searching for trouble. "Number one, I don't know anything about what you brought here. And, B, just so you know, I'm strapped."

"Strapped?" said Chispa, smiling. *This guy watches too much television*, he thought. "Okay. Look, I don't want any trouble. In fact, it's just the opposite. This isn't really my area of expertise. But my boss wants to buy your operation. The whole thing: equipment, inventory, client base, whatever is involved. A one-time lump sum to just walk away."

"Who's your boss?"

Chispa stopped smiling. "He's a very serious man. They all are. That's all you need to know. You should take the deal. Me and you we're probably about the same age. You wouldn't have to work for years."

Tucker snorted out a laugh. "I don't have to work *now*. That's the whole point. How much money are we talking?"

"You're the seller," said Chispa. "What would it take?"

"One point two."

"One point two what?"

"Million," said Tucker. "One point two million."

Chispa reeled back as if he'd been slapped. "You're *loco*, man. It's just *éxtasis*. That's not even close to market value."

"Well, in that case, I think I'm good, bro."

Chispa turned and looked at the fraternity house, the old structure immaculately kept save for the UFOs painted on the windows in shoe polish. The sound of house music reverberated through the back wall. "How old is this house?"

"Uh...well, 1914, so one hundred and five years old. I think."

"Listen, the people I work with. The world I live in. It's not like this." Chispa waved his hand at the house. "I've met some guys like you back home. Trust me. Take some money and move on with your life. This is just fun for you. *Adventuras.* This business is all some people have, and that makes them ruthless. You don't want to get in their way. You also don't want to become them."

"Who the fuck do you think you're talking to?"

"I'm just trying to help, *'mano.* Our people had a man come talk to you?"

Tucker said nothing, puffing out his chest.

"Okay, well that was nobody. I'm nobody. You don't want to see somebody."

"I think it's time you left."

"One hundred thousand cash," said Chispa. "That's the only offer on the table. But I need to see what we're buying first, and you must document the manufacturing process. They need someone on our end to learn how it's made. They don't want quality to suffer."

Chispa handed Tucker the number to his burner phone.

"Think about it. But you only have twenty-four hours. Because that's when they send somebody. And the party's over."

Chispa set down his glass and went inside, leaving Tucker to finish his cigarette on the back porch of the frat house. Then Chispa picked up a paper bag that had been sitting on a nearby table. He looked inside; it contained a box of crackers and a bra.

"Hey," Chispa asked a nearby kid making a house of cards, "Tucker told me to put this in his room. Which one is his?"

"Yeah not many brothers actually live at the house," said the kid without looking up. "Fucking golden boy. Upstairs, fourth door on the right."

"Thank you," said Chispa, walking back to the food and filling a rocket ship-themed paper plate with salami, gouda, ciabata bread, and olives before leaving. On a napkin, he wrote: "Upstairs, fourth door on the right," and stuffed the note in his pocket.

The two buzzcuts at the front door were chatting up a pair of girls dressed as Star Trek red shirts. So, nobody noticed when Chispa left the house just as it started snowing. Folding together a sandwich, he walked toward his hotel into the snowy night.

"Hello?" asked Marilyn Mitchel. "Tucker, are you there?"

"I'm here, Mom." There was an awkward pause as the Hellcat rumbled down 106th Street in East Side. He put his blinker on, slowed and parked in front of the building—right next to Dax's rusted-out Saab with the faded Ron Paul and Infowars stickers.

"It's just that I haven't heard from you in so long."

"What do you want, Mom?"

"Are you...how are you?"

"I'm fine, Mom." Tucker put the car in park and turned it off to save gas.

"I've left several messages over the last few months. I find it hard to believe your own mother doesn't warrant the courtesy you would extend to a stranger." Tucker could tell she was tuning up the tears.

"I've just been busy, Mom. It's nothing personal. Stop being such a drama queen."

"Tuck, we never got a chance to talk after. And I think you know that I don't necessarily agree with your father on his decision. But I need to know what your plans are. We need to talk about things. Can you come by for lunch? Or meet me somewhere?"

"What's to talk about? My plans are the same. I'm finishing out my degree, then I'll put in my time as an analyst somewhere.

Pay my dues as an associate. New York or London. Maybe Asia. Take it from there."

"Yes, but I don't understand. How are you paying for all this? Your father... Well, let's not dress it up, he *cut you off* almost six months ago. How are you living? Paying for school? Fraternity dues? Keeping up that ridiculous car?"

"The question isn't who is going to let me," said Tucker. "It's who is going to stop me."

"Oh, please. Spare me the Masters of the Universe bullshit. I saw the look on your face that day, remember? Wait. Who said that? Who's going to stop me and all that?"

"Ayn Rand, Mom. It's a quote from Ayn Rand."

"Oh, for the love of Christ. You know how they tell corn has matured down in places like Bloomington and Carlinville? They wait until it stops quoting Ayn Rand."

"Well, that's a sentiment, but not an argument. Anyway, I don't want Dad's help and I don't need it, so fuck him. I've got a number of irons in the fire. I've started a pharmaceuticals business. I'm also trying to get an internet gig up and running. Kind of a subscription thing. I'm telling you, as far as I'm concerned, Dad can load that fucking trust into one of those duck-hunting guns and insert it into his ass sideways. Because I'm making shit happen all on my own."

The phone fell silent.

"Mom? You still there?"

"Meet with me, Tucker. Please. I need to know you're alright. How about a quick game of tennis? They just redid the clay courts over at the Racquet Club."

"It's not okay," Tucker said. "What you did. Just *standing* there while he called me lazy and directionless. It's fucked up."

"I beg your pardon? Tucker Davenport Mitchell, you can't talk to me like that. Let me tell you something about your father..."

Tucker tried to see what Dax was doing inside the building, but Dax had not only lowered the inside shade but also closed the outside shutters. Good man.

Tucker let her finish, then said: "Mom, I'm trying to close a big deal with my pharmaceuticals start-up. It's really not a good time for me."

Her heard her breath catch.

"Mom, seriously. Don't cry. I'm fine and I love you and we're going to get together. It's just, not right now. Let me get through this deal and I promise we'll meet. Tennis and lunch. Racquet Club."

"When?"

He ended the call.

"We have to clean up this shithole," Tucker said as he walked inside the building. Pink Floyd's "Dark Side of the Moon" was playing full blast.

Dax was gingerly mixing hydrochloric acid, isopropyl alcohol and an inert cherry flavoring—getting ready to prep for molding into the Corvette press design that made their trademark dissolvable tab so distinctive. Dax raised a finger while he finished the blend. Then he picked up a remote control and turned down the music. "What?" he asked, pulling off his mask.

"I said we have to clean up this shithole." All around them was a jumble of kegs, kettles, tubing, beakers, jugs, hoses, toolboxes, storage bins, computer equipment, and chemical totes. The air tasted bitter.

"What?" Dax raised an eyebrow. "Clean up? Why?"

"We're having company."

Birgit Olson lay on her stiff dorm bed, staring straight up at the ceiling as Dying Darcy explained her fibromyalgia diagnosis and its symptoms. In great detail. Fatigue. Trouble sleeping. Chronic muscle pain.

Going on the second hour, and as Darcy was getting to the details about the complications with her colon, Birgit sat up wordlessly and put on her coat, not bothering with gloves or boots. Darcy never stopped talking as Birgit shouldered her backpack and walked out the door.

The cold air stung but also felt good. She'd cried all night, then gotten very ill and now found the winter air an unexpectedly soothing nostrum. *How could I be so stupid?* she thought. *What, did you think you were just going to meet some random stranger and then your pathetic life would suddenly be awesome? Please. This is fucking Chicago, not a Hallmark movie.*

She sat through three classes—Typography, Visual Branding, and Commercial Design Criticism—without taking a single note. At lunch, she couldn't even think about food but instead took a walk around the campus before her next class. She was past the crying phase and coming to terms with the disappointment of it all. It wouldn't have hurt quite as badly if she hadn't enjoyed the evening so much. At least at first.

Then Birgit began getting angry. *How could he be such an asshole? Should I call the cops? What if he does that to someone else? What if he does worse?*

The long walk helped her think it through. Process it all. At one point, she'd almost convinced herself that the whole thing had been a misunderstanding. That he wasn't really trying to record them having sex. But that wasn't true, and she knew it. He hadn't even called her today; she didn't even warrant that, apparently.

Eventually Birgit glanced at her watch. She'd been walking the campus for an hour, and it was almost time for Intermediate Drawing. Her stomach had settled a bit. *Food is still out of the question*, she thought, *but coffee sounds nice.* She walked hurried past Roasters and ducked into a place called The Bean's List a few doors down. Unwinding her scarf, she fished her wallet from her purse and waited in line.

That's when she saw the poster. It hung on the wall above the cashier, and there was no mistaking the thin, angular face. Tucker Mitchell.

Tucker was dressed in chinos and a fleece sweater—helping a little boy bait his fishing hook at the end of a pier. "Lake

Chums," read the poster's headlines. "Helping bring a smile to boys in need."

"Oh, you have got to be shitting me," said Birgit, balling her fists.

"Hi there," said the girl at the cash register. "Congratulations on making The Bean's List. Would you like to donate a dollar to Lake Chums with your order?"

Birgit started to lash out at the cashier but then caught herself when she remembered something. A plan formed in her mind, like storm clouds taking the shape of an angry animal. And the thought made her very, very happy.

"Hello," said Birgit with a smile. "May I have a Sumatran blend please? Black? And make that to go."

She paid for her coffee and left, walking in the opposite direction from Intermediate Drawing. Over and over, she remembered the cool metal. The sharp precision of that button above the trigger. The feel of the weight in her hand, like the judge's gavel she'd held when her high school civics class visited the Pepin County Courthouse in Wisconsin. Like it held the power to change everything.

El Burro.

Chispa sat in the library, knee-deep in a copy of *A History of Electricity and Magnetism.* He'd found a window seat, the sun's reflection on the snow outside giving him plenty of light. And still, as he held his hand in front of the window, he was amazed that it let in so little cold. The library's heater blew full blast, and if he hadn't been so into his book, he might have fallen asleep like the girl at the table next to him.

He was pulled from blissful reading by his stomach, which made such a violent growl that he feared it would wake the nearby sleeping student.

He hadn't moved, eaten or used the bathroom for hours. He still couldn't believe that anyone could buy a Visiting Researcher

Day Pass at the university's library for twenty-five dollars. Books. Periodicals. Videos. He wanted to just move into the library and never go back. He'd miss Mexico, of course, with the kind of passion only one of his countrymen could understand. But he wouldn't miss the casita with the leaking roof outside of town, constantly threatening to ruin his thin collection of prized engineering books. He wouldn't miss the crushing poverty that's misshapen so many lives around him. And he surely would not miss wasting his intellect as an errand boy for crazies like Dante Garcia.

Chispa has been to Universidad Autónoma de Sinaloa in Los Mochis, and other colleges in Sinaloa. For a time he tortured himself over the prospect of attendance. But without the money, and no parents to help, that was just a dream. Especially given the criminal record that was the price of his meager existence with the Sangre Cartel.

I have to be realistic, he thought, closing the book. *I have a job to do, if I want a future at all. And it's not like I can check myself out of El Patrón's crew like a library book.* He stood and stretched. Then with more sadness than he'd known in a long time, he left the books where they lay and stepped out into the bitter cold.

Chispa walked west. It was almost two hours before he found what he was looking for: a big, white IT&T utility van parked halfway in the splotchy grass of a home in Auburn Gresham. With no sign of the driver, he took a quick look around and opened the door. The van chimed pleasantly, and he slid inside. The cabin was still warm.

Removing a screwdriver from his sweatshirt, Chispa popped the housing off the steering column and went to work. A few minutes later, he was driving back toward the university with the heater on full blast. *When I get back home,* he thought, *I am going to lay out on the beach at Playa Olas Altas for a week. And drink hot coffee.*

He drove the van back to Fosforo's as quickly as he could

without drawing attention, careful to use his turn signals, stop completely and follow every sign best he could. He liked America so far, but it seemed like there was a new rule hiding around every corner waiting to bite you like a snake.

"I need a driver," Chispa explained to Fosforo.

Fosforo had a Ford Raptor with Michigan Plates up on a lift at Consolidated Auto Care. He was helping three other guys remove the transmission. *Los Tigres del Norte* blared in the background and the shop's air hung thick with the scent of skunkweed.

"To take care of this alternator problem," said Chispa continued. "I need a driver. Told the poor guy we were going to buy him out. Distracted him with a fake deadline. I'll handle it today when he's not expecting it. I feel bad. He's my age."

"Yeah, well, that poor college kid is costing Dante Garcia money. And Dante Garcia don't like that. He don't much like you, either. You want backup?"

"Nah, just a driver. All he has to do is just ride with me and then drive this van somewhere it will disappear. Chorro, anyone. But we need to hurry because any minute they'll report the van stolen. Then bad things will happen."

Fosforo laughed. "Bad things always happen, *empollón*. That's why we get paid the big bucks. We in the Bad Things Happening business."

Fosforo stepped out from under the truck and whistled. "Bulldog."

A thin man at a bench nearby set down a grinding tool and lifted his safety glasses. He had four teardrops tattooed on his face and a long scar running the length of his cheek.

"Go with this man. He needs a driver. Be back inside the hour. Those two Hondas go out today and I don't want to hear any of your bullshit." The man nodded wordlessly and removed his glasses.

A few minutes later, Chispa pulled the van into the small driveway at Tau Theta Alpha house. There was no missing the enormous IT&T logo and bright yellow cherry-picker bucket on top. He put the vehicle in park.

"Okay, wait until I wave and then go," said Chispa. "I need them to see this van." He took an IT&T cap, a black duffle bag and a metal clipboard full of papers off the dash and got out of the driver's side door. On his way to the front door of the frat house, he jammed the cap low on his head.

Bulldog slid over and got behind the wheel.

When Chispa knocked on the door, he was surprised to see a plump *tia* answer.

"Yes?"

Chispa removed the IT&T cap. "Hello. Sorry to disturb you but we've had reports of the internet running slow at this address. I just need to come in and check some things. We're doing the whole block."

"If you work for IT&T," said the woman, "how come you're wearing a Star Trek sweatshirt?"

"They called me on my day off just to come fix this problem. Customer service is our Number 1 priority at IT&T."

She leaned out to see the big bucket truck in the driveway. "Okay, well, mind the floors," she said, opening the door and waving Chispa inside. "It's bad enough cleaning after these heathens all day, much as I love them."

Chispa waved at Bulldog, who backed out of the driveway.

All around the world, he thought, *people think their internet should be faster.*

Chispa found the cable run in the big media room, actually performing a speed test with some equipment he'd found in the duffle: 43.1 Mbps download speed. *Meh. Dante Garcia's satellite is faster*, Chispa thought, *if you don't mind the chance that a bullet could take you offline permanently.*

Then, for the purposes of believability, and just having a look around at who was there, he went outside a few times to "look for a cable run," always careful to take off his shoes when he came back inside. Only a few students were in the house, one studying in the kitchen and another playing a video game in a small den. No Tucker Mitchell. No buzzcuts.

The *tia* returned to a front room where she was organizing stacks of papers. After a few minutes, he waited for the *tia* to leave the front room and then slammed the front door. Then, shoes in hand, he snuck upstairs careful to avoid anyone's notice.

He stepped into the fourth room on the right. It was tidy with a small bed, a few computers and a polished wooden desk. After searching the room thoroughly, he determined that he could easily climb out the window, onto the roof and down a nearby tree when the job was done. Feeling better about his escape, he opened the folding closet doors and pushed the clothes aside. They smelled like body spray. Then he squatted down and pulled the closet doors closed. Lastly, he removed his leather belt, wrapped one end around his right hand, and waited— watching through the slats in the closet door.

Waiting for his prey.

Since she'd left the dorm without her gloves, Birgit's fingers were numb with cold.

I don't want to hurt him, she thought. *Just teach him a lesson.*

She knew she wasn't thinking clearly. It was like the sensation of realizing you're dreaming in the middle of a dream. *I should just take a few days off and go back home. Pick up a bumbleberry pie and spend the weekend licking my wounds. Listen to Dad talk about the morning's fishing or Mom complain about the neighbor's goats; build a* gardesgard *around myself and emerge when I'm whole again.*

But she couldn't stop herself. Something in her had broken and, if she was honest, it wasn't just about Tucker or last night. It was about hating this place. Being alone. Worse, *feeling* alone. Birgit had never been overly dependent. She didn't need a friend to go with her when she bought clothes; she was happy to attend parties alone but wasn't crushed when not invited. She had good friends, lots of them, but none nearby. And that matters; more than she'd thought. *All of these people in the city*, she thought, *and nobody cares. Nobody.* Now she felt like that place inside her, that well she could drink from when the world was indifferent, had been too dry for too long. There was nothing staring back at her when she looked down in there.

And, now, nobody to stop her.

At the TTA house, she waited until a boy was coming in, then fell into place behind him.

"Thanks," she said with a smile as he held the door.

"Sure," said the boy, running off to the kitchen.

The house looked banal; stuffy even, in the daylight. Gone were any traces of last night's Alien Invasion. And the place was practically empty.

She'd started for the stairs when a voice called out.

"Can I help you?"

Whirling around, Birgit saw a woman in her forties sorting papers at a long table in the front room. "Oh, hi." she said. "Um, I was at the party last night and I left my gloves upstairs. My fingers are positively glacial."

The woman took off her reading glasses, scowling. "Do you know which room?"

"Yes, ma'am. Fourth door on the right. Tucker's room."

"Oh," the woman said, warming into a grin. "Well all right, dear. Let me know if you can't find them."

"I will. Thank you."

If I'm really quiet, Birgit thought as she walked up the stairs, *I can just wait up there for him. When he comes in, we'll have a little video session of our own. Because he has some confessing to do with the help from* El Burro.

* * *

97

Chispa had just started to doze when a girl walked into the room, closing the door behind her.

"Tucker?" she called in a whisper. "Tuck, are you in here?"

She looked familiar. But he couldn't quite place the face. After stopping to listen, she walked to the desk, opened the drawer and pulled out *El Burro*. Chispa's blood ran cold when she looked right at him.

It's so weird, she thought. *I can still feel the camera on me— recording through that damn closet door.* She felt as if someone were staring at her right now. *Hopefully*, Birgit thought as she walked slowly toward the closet, *the woman downstairs will forget about me, or come up to check and not bother looking in here.*

At the closet, she placed her hand upon the knob, pausing to listen for anyone coming down the hallway. Then she threw open the door.

The camera was gone.

In its place was a man.

Eyes wide, knees tucked up to his chest, he had a belt wrapped around his hand.

Screaming, Birgit raised the gun and pulled the trigger as fast as she could.

Chispa stood straight up when the girl opened the closet door, hitting his head on the clothes bar and seeing stars.

Rubbing his noggin, he stumbled from the closet—the metallic clicking of *El Burro* repeating as Birgit pulled the trigger over and over.

"What are you doing, *vieja loca?*" Chispa hissed, snatching the gun from Birgit's hands.

The girl looked pale as a *vampiro*. She stopped screaming, opening her mouth but not quite forming words. For a second,

Chispa couldn't find his duffle. He pulled it out of the closet and stuffed *El Burro* inside. He'd put his belt back on and was fumbling with the buckle when the door flew open.

It was the *tia*, flanked by two of the boys who'd been downstairs.

"What in the love of God is going on?" asked the woman.

Chispa smiled. "I think I startled this young lady," he said.

"Dude, did you show her your junk or something?" asked one of the boys.

"What?" said Chispa. "No, no. I had to take off my belt for a waist harness earlier."

"I didn't realize there was anyone up here," said the girl. "I'm sorry I screamed."

"I didn't realize *either of you* were still here," said the *tia*. "And why is Tucker's closet open?"

"I was looking for the coax feed in this room."

"Duh," said the other boy, pointing to the computer by Tucker's bed. "It's right there, dumb ass. How did you not see that?"

"Thad," said the *tia*. "Language."

"Sorry Mrs. P."

"Where are your gloves, young lady?"

"They...they weren't here. I guess I was mistaken. Sorry to bother you." She all but ran from the room. It was then that Chispa placed her as the girl who'd knocked him over at the party.

He closed the closet door. "I need to go test something at the property next door," Chispa said. "I may or may not be back depending on the result."

The *tia* and the two boys stared at him as he made his way down the stairs and out the door.

Between the cold wind and tears, Birgit wasn't making much progress. She was only two blocks away when the man caught up with her.

"Pardon me, miss?"

She walked faster as he drew closer. *This is what I get*, she thought. *Play stupid games, win stupid prizes. All I wanted was to spend a night doing something besides listening to Darcy complain about her make-believe asthma. Now I'm going to be strangled with a belt by the cable guy.*

"Miss, please, wait."

She spun around quickly, slipping on the ice of the sidewalk and reaching out wildly.

He took her elbow, keeping her upright.

She didn't want it. She hated the thought of it. But she couldn't help it. She burst into tears in the middle of the sidewalk. One final good cry over the whole incident.

Burying her head in the stranger's chest, she felt like a drowning person—grasping at anyone nearby in desperation. And the fact that she didn't have the power to stop it made her angry, which made the tears came harder. He smelled like cigarette smoke and spearmint gum.

The man put an arm around her gingerly, letting her cry for a minute and smiling uncomfortably at passersby. When the worst of it had gone, she stood up straight and wiped at her eyes with cold fingers. "I am so sorry," she said, drawing a ragged breath. "I'm...I'm just not myself today. I mean, what was I thinking? What was I doing?"

She tried to wipe a smudge of mascara off his sweatshirt. It was a hoodie sporting the original Star Trek cast in uniform on the transporter deck, glowing in mid beam. The word *Energize!* was written across the top.

"Hey," said the man, who looked to be about her age. "Do you know a good pizza place?"

At Nick & Vito's Pizzeria, Birgit's hands shook as she lifted the beer to her lips. The waitress set a combo basket of mushrooms, poppers, zucchini and onion rings on the table. The restaurant was warm and smelled delicious. *Pizza*, thought Chispa. *That's another thing people everywhere agree on.*

"My God, what did I almost do?" asked Birgit.

She put her head in her hands. "I swear I'm not a crazy person."

"You're being too hard on yourself," said Chispa. "What's so crazy about sneaking into a fraternity house and trying to shoot the cable guy?" He smiled.

"I just don't know what got into me," Birgit said. "I was so angry."

"Love makes people do funny things," said Chispa. "So I've been told." He reached into his jeans pocket and came out with a handful of .45 rounds, pouring them onto the table.

Birgit slapped her hand onto the bullets to keep them from rolling off the table. "I am so sorry," she said. "I can't believe I behaved in such an irrational and irresponsible way. And it wasn't love. Trust me. Just...I don't know, loneliness."

She explained what happened the night before—at first feeling a bit embarrassed, but then buoyed up by the fact that she hadn't done anything wrong other than trust a creep. Also, she didn't know this cable guy at all. Sometimes it's easy to tell your problems to a complete stranger you'll never see again.

"Wow," said Chispa. "I'm sorry that happened to you. All is forgiven. I mean, even if it weren't, I'd tell you that it was. After all, I've seen what you're capable of." Again, he smiled, like it had been a joke just between the two of them. Which it was.

She laughed and crossed her arms. "So, what's your story? What kind of cable guy steals bullets from someone's gun and hides in their closet?"

"It's complicated," he said. "And kind of depressing."

"That's sketchy."

"I know."

"I remember you. I ran into you on my way-out last night. Tau Theta Alphas invite all of their cable guys to theme parties?"

"I've got a side business," he said, winking. He threw out a few things about working for IT&T which sounded right to him, and he hinted around that he sold the college boys weed. But the lies soured in his mouth. Felt wrong. He liked this girl. Respected her, despite the frantic state in which they'd met. They talked about Chicago, Star Trek, which Grand Theft Auto version was the best, and their hometowns. He talked about his passion for electronics.

Eventually, Birgit took out her computer and showed him her graphic design portfolio project—a series of themed infographics focused on the impact of technology in our everyday lives. Chispa thought it interesting and was startled by her talent. It was beautiful and fascinating work.

But he had a problem, and he couldn't allow himself to be distracted.

What am I going to do now? he thought. *My whole plan was to set up a fake meeting with Tucker Mitchell and catch him beforehand, off-guard. Surely word of the strange cable man and the nosy ex-girlfriend would get back to him. He'd be on guard. And Dante Garcia's patience was no doubt thinning.*

Chispa had only $318 left—just enough to pay for one more night at the Tony Hyde Park Hotel, today's pizza, and a few odds and ends before he left. He felt like one of the free divers in Playa del Carmen, in awe of the beauty around them but also holding their breath in terror.

He listened to Birgit talk about the infographics on the screen of her laptop, and what they represented. The pale sunlight from the snowy streets outside gave her hair and skin a brilliant glow. Bloodshot as they were, her eyes burned with intelligence. He tried to focus on what she was saying, but was distracted by his mind, churning in circles trying to get a sense of her; taking in all the fascinating details.

"I'm probably boring you with this stuff," she said, dipping a fried zucchini slice into some ranch dressing and popping it into her mouth.

"Not at all," he said. "I guess I really never thought about how things like that are made. What's this one about?"

Chispa pointed to a picture of a car's dashboard. Where the gauges should go, each had a small graphic displaying various statistics.

She clicked on the image, making it bigger. "The internet of things as relates to the automotive industry," she said. "By 2020, hundreds of millions of cars will be connected to the internet. That's going to change a lot of things for a lot of people. Of, course it won't change much for me. I sold my car when I moved down here."

Chispa studied the graphic. One little icon, a fedora with a pair of sunglasses, was labeled Digital Security Concerns. "The average car has more than thirty computers," it read, "opening up serious concerns about vehicle hacking and privacy."

"Oh, that's so true," he said, pointing to the security stat. "About cars and computers." Then he told her some of the things he'd done to modify cars for his friends back in Mexico—glossing over the fact that most of his "customers" were homicidal drug lords. He also didn't explain how he'd gotten to Chicago. She didn't ask.

The pizza was thin with a cracker-like crust. Chispa had never tasted anything like it, and he ate almost half immediately. He had to make himself stop, though he could have easily eaten the rest. Listening to Birgit talk, the same sense of dread overcame him that he felt at the library. Soon it would be time to go back home to his life back in Mexico—back to doing the bidding of the Sangre Cartel and the likes of Dante Garcia.

So she'd tried to shoot him earlier? He liked her. A lot. But that would have to wait; maybe forever. He had a problem to solve. A delicate problem within a complicated system.

Chispa wiped his mouth and placed his napkin in his plate. "I have to get back to work," he said. He stood and placed a fifty on the table. "I hope you feel better."

"Thank you," she said, standing and holding out her hand.

They shook. Then there was an awkward pause before Chispa turned to go.

"Wait, take these," she said, pointing to the bullets.

"Keep them. I'll hang on to 'El Burro.' Maybe we can get together sometime in the future and put your roommate out of her misery," he said with a wink.

She burst out laughing. "Well give me your number, then. You know, so we can arrange things with the hit. She thinks she has mono now, so she'll be an easy target."

"Maybe you really are crazy," he said, scrawling down the number to the burner phone Fosforo had given him. "Call me when you're feeling yourself and we can talk about how much better an actor Patrick Stewart is than William Shatner."

"Blasphemy," she called out after him, as he walked out of the pizza joint and into the blowing snow.

To save money, Chispa walked back to the hotel from Nick & Vito's. Along the way, he thought about his failed attempt to take care of Tucker. He thought about the library and how much he'd enjoyed himself. And, of course, he thought about her.

Back at the hotel, he turned the room's heater up as warm as it would go. Then he fired up his laptop. He opened up a new tab in his computer's Tor browser and went to Google. Then he typed "Electronics Schematic, Dodge Hellcat."

Flip the pledge was at the TTA house's mammoth dining hall table eating a bowl of Cinnamon Toast Crunch and pecking away at a sociology paper on Perceived Organizational Risks and Their Relationship to Individual Conformity.

Chad Lewis walked calmly into the room, closed Flip's laptop, picked it up and dropped it neatly into a nearby trashcan.

Flip held out his arms. "What the fuck, dude? That's due today."

"Sorry," said Chad. "Guess you should have thought about that before you went to the beach."

"Went to the beach?"

"Yeah. Went to the beach. Forgot something. Slacked off.

Now you're going to mouth off too?"

"Seriously, man. I don't know what you're talking about."

"Clearly not." Chad crooked his finger at Flip. "Over here."

Flip got up and followed Chad out of the room, bending down to retrieve his laptop from the trash can along the way.

Chad walked them into the garage. The space had five bay doors for five cars—a privilege reserved for brothers who went the extra mile as decided by a High Five Committee at the end of each month.

Icy wind whipped huge snowflakes around inside the garage, a lone red plastic cup bouncing around the floor. An inch of white covered half the floor and the rear of each vehicle.

"Oh, shit," said Flip.

"That's right. Oh shit. Because whose job is it to close the garage doors?"

"Whoever uses the garage."

"Correct. And whose job is it to make sure all five people parked in the garage comply with that rule? And, on top of that, who does the Sergeant at Arms rely on to make sure the house is locked up tight each night?"

"The pledges."

"That's right. The pledges."

"Sorry, Chad. But I checked the garage last night. Everyone was in for the night and the doors were all closed."

"Do they look closed? Seems to me like they've been open all damn night. And get that look of martyrdom off your face; I'm trying to help you, bro. Because shit would have hit the fan if something would've happened to any of these cars while the garage doors were open. Especially," Chad pointed at the Hellcat "that one." He made a gun with his finger and pointed it at Flip, mouthing the words "*El Burro.*"

Flip swallowed hard, punching a button on the garage wall. The metal doors buzzed slowly downward, the red plastic cup finally coming to rest beneath a framed Mumford & Sons poster.

* * *

Upstairs in his room, Tucker made the call. He'd been up all night thinking about it. Now he just wanted to get the transaction over with.

"Okay, a hundred grand," he said when the man answered. "Cash. And you know you're getting a deal." To be honest, Tuck wasn't going to miss being the kingpin of Route 66 ecstasy. Selling out would get Bryce off his back, fund the remainder of school and set him up for a little while wherever he interned. A *very little* while if it were New York or London but, still, it would be a start.

Tuck listened to the man on the other end of the phone, slipping on a pair of L.L. Bean Duck Boots and looking for his keys. He gave the odds of this guy Chispa being a narc at around fifty-fifty. But if that were the case, he was going down anyway. And it if he weren't, he'd be solid and set for a while. Besides, he figured he'd better get comfortable with managing high-stakes risk if trading were his future.

"Yeah," Tucker told Chispa. "We're in East Side. Hundred and Sixth Street." Tucker gave him directions and pocketed his keys. "Meet me there in an hour."

"Oh, and just so you know," Tucker added, "we take security very seriously. So, mind your manners, bro." He ended the call and walked to his desk.

Opening the middle drawer, he was faced with a folded-up copy of *The Economist,* a fistful of pens, his checkbook, a pocket version of Wealth of Nations, a pair of knock-off Jim Beam Ray Bans he'd been given at a golf tournament, and a box of rubbers.

But no *El Burro.*

"What the shit?"

He dug through the drawer, frantically. Playing cards. Highlighter. Dog whistle.

No gun.

Tucker stood straight up. *Who's been through my desk? And when?* When he first got *El Burro* he admitted to making a habit of checking on it periodically. Just to make himself feel better. Fidgeting with it while he talked on the phone. Using the grip to crack walnuts. And, one time, he was ashamed to admit, posing in front of the mirror with it like an extra in the old Lee Marvin show *M Squad*.

Then it came to him. *Bryce Graham. Had to be. Chad and Flip were with me when I bought it, so why would they care? Bryce was probably snooping around his room looking for Route 66 when he saw it. He took it and now he must be preparing to kick me out. Fuck*

Throwing on his Patagonia vest, he went downstairs.

Bryce was drinking coffee with Blane Everett, having a heated debate involving Jay Cutler's career yardage.

"Hey," Tucker said to Bryce on the way to the garage. "So, we've got something to talk about later, huh?"

Bryce set his coffee down, a blank look on his face. "Oh, yeah? What's up?"

"I think you know," Tuck said, slamming the door to the garage behind him.

Bryce and Blane fell silent, looking at the door. Then they looked at each other and shrugged in unison. "So, anyway, don't forget about that run game, bitch. Detroit Lions in 2009. Play fake, runs it—breaks the plane in mid-air Blackhawk Down style. Booyah." The two clinked coffee cups.

In the garage, Tucker fired up the Hellcat and punched the garage door open. The gauges lit, moving all the way right before settling back down to idle, the thunderous exhaust echoing through the small space. Technically, he still shouldn't be driving the Hellcat in snowy conditions. But he just couldn't help himself. As usual.

Using the car's rear camera, he backed out into the street.

Why is there snow all over my rear windshield? he thought. But he had a lot on his mind and didn't think much about it. Tucker had driven to the building in East Side so many times over the last few months, he hardly had to think about it. Even in the snow.

"Hey, Siri," he said, once he was on his way. "Call Dax."

"*Cawling Dox*," said the female voice in a posh, British Home Counties accent. Tucker liked setting it on the British female setting. Thought it sounded "all *Downton Abbey* and shit."

Dax picked up on the third ring. "Hello."

"Hey, man. I'm bringing that dude I was telling you about over to the shop. I think he's going to buy us out."

"Oh, no shit?"

"Yeah. Fifty thousand bucks. And we'll split it right down the middle."

"Word. I made him a recipe book like you asked."

"Cool. Hey, do me a favor will you? I don't want him thinking we're just a couple of bitches and walking all over us, negotiation-wise. Do you think you could sort of make yourself look a little harder than usual?"

"Harder?"

"Yeah, you know. Tougher. Like maybe not wear your glasses when he's there. Put on a black shirt or something. Better yet a hat—like Breaking Bad."

"I'm not comfortable with that. I'm a pacifist. Besides, tough isn't really my role. I'm in production. Nobody cares how tough the chef is at Everest. They only care how buttery the *Sole Meunière* tastes."

"Humor me. I'm not asking you to enter the octagon. Just try not to look like such a fucking dork."

Tucker ended the call. Then he tapped the Hellcat's dash screen and put on some music; Limp Bizkit with "Break Stuff." "*...right now I'm dangerous...*" Tucker tapped the steering wheel to the beat, whipping off his Ray Bans to clean off a speck of dirt.

He took it easy on the car, careful in the snow—which blew sideways in the wind. He drove down South Cottage Grove. Though Cottage Grove Heights. Past Gately Park, the Harborside Golf Course and Railroad Marsh.

On 103rd coming up to the "T" intersection at S. Torrence Avenue, he tapped the brakes ahead of the light.

The Hellcat didn't respond.

Tucker hit the brake again, this time with more pressure.

Still nothing.

The engine's idle gradually increased. Gripping the steering wheel, Tucker stomped on the brakes as hard as he could. The dashboard went dark, then lit up again.

Suddenly he was pushed back into the seat as the engine roared up to 4,000 RPM, then shifted gears. The slick racing tires spun on the wet asphalt, then gradually found purchase.

Panicking, Tucker turned the wheel, the car swerving left, then right. A FedEx van in the opposing lane dodged the Hellcat, running up on the curb and barely missing a tree. The sound of its honking warped as Tuck's car flew by.

The Hellcat's engine revved again, launching Tucker into S. Torrence Street beneath the red light. Eyes wide, Tucker instinctively lowered his head a little. Looking right, the coast was clear. Looking left, Tucker worked hard to process what he was seeing.

Time slowed, the song on the radio screwing down to a warped half-speed.

It was a man with a moustache and fat, sloppily knotted tie. He sat in an impossibly large enclosure. The front was made mostly of glass. Bright yellow letters above the driver's head read: "Crosstown." The light inside the vehicle seemed preternaturally bright against the glum winter's day. *A bus. It was a bus*, Tucker thought. Coming right at him.

He locked eyes with the driver briefly. Then the bus driver threw his hands in front of his face. Tucker instinctively pulled right inside his seatbelt, like a batter trying to avoid getting hit by a wayward baseball pitcher.

He thought of his mother.

The impact echoed throughout South Chicago. The bus shuddered with the impact, its massive rear raising up and then bouncing crookedly and skidding with an awkward *ruk-ruk-ruk* squeal. Something metal came off and rolled across the street, bouncing into a nearby vacant lot. The Hellcat folded sideways into a fiery V, scraping and skidding as it was pushed a half-block down S. Torrence in a storm of twisting metal, melting plastic and tinkling glass. People at a nearby church hit the ground, thinking a bomb had gone off. Thick, black smoke spewed from the wreck like an oilfield fire.

A man in Bulls jersey filling up an El Camino at the BP on the corner set his forty-ounce beer on the hood of his car and ran to the sidewalk for a closer look. Squinting into the flames, he took his cigarette out of his mouth and said. "Damn son. Y'all see that shit?"

Chispa closed his laptop. He was in a nearby fried chicken joint, a copy of *The Car Hacker's Guidebook* on the table. He'd had a leisurely lunch of lake perch and spicy chicken wings slathered in red sauce, washing it all down with a liter of Grape Crush. Then he'd bided his time until the GPS locator he'd placed on Tucker's car last night had put the Hellcat in a favorable spot for the task at hand.

In all his time with the Sangre Cartel, he'd only killed two other people personally—both when he was very young. That was before the organization had discovered his true talents. And not a night had gone by when he didn't see both of those men in his sleep. He didn't want to think about all of the things he'd fixed which led to other deaths: satellite phones, computers, wiretaps, and countless other toys. *And now I'll have one or two more souls to face each night*, he thought. *But, one way or the other, I am out.*

He'd planned to walk up S. Torrence and see the damage for himself. However, the black smoke rising above the rail yard told him everything needed to know. So instead he walked south toward 106th Street and the address Tucker Mitchell had given him.

It was a boarded-up building with shutters on the windows and a Saab parked out front. Someone had spray painted "Free Self Defense Lessons. Just Pull Out Money and Wait" on the side of the building. Chispa knocked.

An overweight man in a black shirt opened the door, leaning close to squint at him.

"Can I help you?" he asked.

"Yes. I'm the guy Tucker told you about. From Mexico."

"Oh, hi," said the man, squinting harder to look around the parking lot.

"I'm Dax. Where's Tucker?"

"He's not going to make it, but he wanted me to come by and get the book as well as any remaining inventory."

"Okay," said the man, opening the door. Chispa stepped in. Pink Floyd's "Dark Side of the Moon" was playing.

"I think I should call Tucker."

"Is this the book?" Chispa asked, pointing at an outsized leather notebook in the middle of a cluttered workbench.

"Yes, actually. Hang on." Dax pulled out his phone, squinting to make a call.

Chispa took the opportunity to look around the small open plan building, including a storage room and a bathroom. There was nobody else around. He looked in one of the boxes in the back-storage room. There were thousands of Route 66 tabs.

"Voicemail," said Dax, suddenly appearing by Chispa's side. "I'm not sure you should be back here."

Chispa removed *El Burro* from his waistband. "Okay, here's the deal. I need you to give me your car keys and just walk away from the building."

"I'm sorry," he said, half a smile on his face.

"In five minutes, some very serious men are going to arrive and pack this whole place up into a series of boxes. You need to be gone by then. If you are still here, you will be one of the things that goes into a box." Chispa racked a .45 bullet into the slide of *El Burro*.

The smile fell from Dax's face. Fumbling around the work-table, he brought out a pair of thick, rectangular glasses. "Righty-ho," he said, putting on the glasses and picking a Star-bucks cup off the worktable. "Keys are by the book." The door made an electronic *bling-blong* as Dax left.

As quickly as he could, Chispa loaded the Saab with all of the Route 66 he could find. He also found $5,000 cash in an ice chest hidden in Dax's Saab along with four pounds of weed and several bricks of hash. He still heard sirens in the distance, though black smoke no longer streaked the sky, as he pulled the beat-up Saab onto 106th Street.

Fosforo pulled his Escalade up to Consolidated Auto Care in Riverdale at five in the morning the next day to find a pile of boxes in front of the office door. *Que mierda?* he thought. *I get a delivery already?* Back in the day, Fosforo did overnight hot-shot runs of stolen auto parts in Mexico City—where he learned to get up early. So, nobody at Consolidated ever arrived before he did unless they slept in the back.

He got out and rolled up one of the bay doors, eyeballing the pile of boxes under the overhang in front of the office. Then he parked the Escalade in the garage and walked back to the office door. He counted fourteen boxes total. A note was duct taped on top. "Alternator Problem Solved. Driving back to Sinaloa today.—Chispa."

"Fucking *empollón*," Fosforo said, looking around. Aside from one lone homeless man warming himself by a barrel fire across the street, he was by himself under the sickly yellow streetlight. He pulled a butterfly knife out of his boot, twirled it around and sliced open one of the boxes. Using the blade, he cautiously opened the lid and held his phone up to the box for extra light.

Hundreds of tiny baggies were inside, each containing a small tab with the image of a red Corvette and the words "Route 66." *Que padre*, he said, flipping the knife closed and picking up the open box.

As he was about to carry it inside, he noticed the homeless guy across the way had left his barrel and was approaching.

"I seen the whole thing, mayne," said the guy.

Fosforo took a step back and set the box down. Then he pulled the knife back out, flipping it open. The blade shimmered in the streetlight. "Don't come no closer," Fosforo said.

"Naw, it's cool mayne. I just wanted you to know I saw the whole thing. Shit was *fucked up*, mayne."

"What the fuck you talkin' about?"

"The dude that brought these boxes, mayne. I seen him get jacked by three motherfuckers in a Buick. They fucked that boy *up*, mayne."

"What?"

"Yeah, see. I's right across the street, see. And this dude rolled up and unloaded all these boxes. Then, as he was gettin' back in his ride these three *other guys* came and put a beatin' on him. Snatched his skinny ass up, mayne."

"That makes no sense," said Fosforo. "Why would someone do that?"

"What am I a sociologist, motherfucker? I just seen what I done seen. Bein' a good citizen and shit."

"Was the guy with the boxes alone?"

"Yeah."

"And three guys jumped him?"

"Yeah. In a Buick. Black or dark blue or some shit. It's been snowing like a motherfucker all night, so it was hard to tell. I know because I been out in it freezin' my ass off every minute."

Fosforo tried doing the math in his head but got lost. Who would take Chispa, the nerdy ass *empollón*? Nobody even knows Chispa around here. Hell, nobody knows Chispa back home. Was it the kid who made Route 66? If that were the case, why didn't he take back his inventory? He shook his head to clear it and decided to consider the situation further inside—with some hot coffee and tequila.

"Okay, thanks," Fosforo told the man, who was staring at the ground. Fosforo flicked his knife closed and put it back in his boot.

"Say," said the shabbily dressed man. "Spare a buck for my trouble? I done came over away from my warm barrel to let you know what's up a'ight?"

"Here," said Fosforo, peeling off a twenty. "You see any of those guys around here again, let me know."

"A'ight, mayne." He shuffled back across the street. The hobo stoked his barrel fire with a broken golf club he'd found in the street. As he warmed his fingers, he tried to decide the most judicious way to spend the twenty Fosforo had given him—as well as the hundred dollars the skinny man had given him earlier for watching the boxes and fabricating that story.

Chipsa and Birgit had met in the afternoon for Polish sausage sandwiches from Jim's Original on Maxwell Street, followed by a Star-Trek themed show at Adler Planetarium. Then coffee at Wormhole, where Chispa had come clean and told her everything about his past. He expected her to be horrified, but she just squeezed his hand and said she was sorry. They talked for hours.

It was almost ten by then, and they walked along Navy Pier. The shimmering blackness of the lake sprawled out before them; behind them a glowing neon Ferris wheel churned slowly before the dazzling downtown skyline. They held hands.

"So now that you've managed a clean break, what's next?" she asked.

"I haven't figured out the details yet, but I'm staying. In America. I'm going to study electrical engineering."

"Oh, that's great. Seems perfect for you."

"I'm not gonna lie, I'm scared. I want it so bad that the prospect of messing it all up and getting sent back home is terrifying. Not that I don't love home, but if I went back to study there, I'd live in fear someone would recognize me. That *Sangre* would put me back to work. I'm an orphan, not a slave. And I'm willing to do whatever it takes to keep my freedom. Surely America needs people who can fix things."

"Oh, yeah," she said. "There's plenty over here needs fixing. And, hey, if it helps on the documentation front—I have mad Photoshop skills."

He stopped and looked out over the skyline for a moment. Then he said, "C'mon. There's something I need to do."

Chispa guided Birgit back up the pier, past all the shops and restaurants and the Shakespeare Theatre. Past Crystal Gardens. Past a little park holding a free concert by a Smashing Pumpkins cover band that played "Bullet with Butterfly Wings."

Then he walked her south toward the more deserted piers. Away from the crowd. Away from the light. He found the blackest spot along the water's edge beneath a thin clump of trees. Chispa made sure the trees stood between them and the crowded pier.

Then he pulled out *El Burro*, laying it flat in his hand as if weighing the gun.

The golden pistol shimmered. The diamond in the donkey's tooth sparkled in the moonlight.

Birgit looked at the gun, and at him, her breath slowing. She realized she was the only person who now knew all his secrets. Nobody here knew of his past. Nobody back in Sinaloa knew about his present or future.

"A burro," said Chispa. "Is a beast of burden."

Chispa thought about what Fosforo had said about them being in the Bad Things Happening business. It was true. If he wanted to live, much less have a shot at happiness, he needed a new line of work.

He reared back and flung the gun into the water as far he could. It landed with a satisfying *ker-plunk*. "I'm done carrying other people's baggage."

She wrapped her arms around him and pulled him close as they stared out at the water.

As they walked back toward the crowd hand-in-hand, the band in the park played a cover of "Landslide."

"You know," she said, "I've been thinking about getting a new roommate."

"Really? Well, ideally you need one who can help pay the bills."

"Sure," she said. "Or, you know, someone willing to work off the debt. With things that need seeing to around the house." She gave Chipsa a look that made him blush.

"Come to think of it," said Chispa. "I should actually apply at IT&T. I could set up routers and run fiber optic with my eyes closed."

"Great. There goes my indentured manservant fantasy."

"I wonder what kind of paperwork I'd need, exactly? Tell me about these Photoshop skills of yours."

And so they walked—just two more dreamers at Navy Pier. Walking under the pale moon, high in the night as a pop fly at Wrigley Field. Walking under the 20,000 mega-watts of Midwestern electricity that would become Chispa's artist medium. Walking towards who-knows-what but warmed by the kind of heat you need to pack inside you at all times to survive Chicago. Taking aim at the whole damn city. Together.

GUNS + TACOS · CREATED AND EDITED BY   MICHAEL BRACKEN & TREY R. BARKER

JAMES A. HEARN

A BERETTA, BURRITOS AND BEARS

SEASON **1**   GUNS + TACOS   EPISODE **6**

A BERETTA, BURRITOS, AND BEARS

James A. Hearn

September 17, 2018, 6:22 p.m.
South Deering, Chicago

Brian Piccolo reached for the woman in his dream, his hands clutching a dirty pillow and drawing it tightly against his chest. Her milk-white skin was velvet-smooth, her freckled nose inches from his own. He caught the scent of freshly cut apples in her fiery red hair.

In the dream, they were sitting on a checkered blanket in a meadow strewn with wildflowers, and bees danced lazily upon a breeze carrying a hint of the summer to come. Farther down the hillside, Buster barked and cavorted in the sun. The yellow Lab's nose was to the ground, his ever-active tail wagging.

Brian turned to the woman and stroked her cheek. This was the place he'd asked Cassidy O'Connor to marry him, many years ago.

"I love you, Cass," Brian murmured. "Thanks for waiting for me."

"And I love you, my darling husband." Cassidy brushed his face with her fingertips and kissed the cleft of his chin.

A shudder of revulsion ran through Brian's body. Something about the way her fingers scuttled across his face filled him with loathing, and his mouth tasted of bile.

"What's wrong, Brian?" asked Cassidy. Her red mouth was twisted into a wicked smile as her fingers played roughly across his forehead. "Don't you love me?"

Brian opened his mouth to reply, to tell her he loved her more than anything in the world, but her coarse fingers slipped inside his lips, gagging him.

They were suddenly naked. Cassidy flipped him on his back, her fingers in his mouth controlling him like a horse's bit. She mounted him roughly, trapping him between her muscular thighs, her legs squeezing the air from his lungs.

"Fuck me."

"Cass, I can't breathe," he gasped.

She rode him hard, her breasts bouncing rhythmically, eyes closed in ecstasy. Her legs tightened their grip with each downward plunge.

"Cass...you're...killing me!"

In Cassidy's moan of climax, Brian felt his life slipping away. He was no longer in the meadow on the hill, in their special place, but drifting down into a dark and moldering grave. He looked up to see Cassidy's face far above him, framed in a shrinking rectangle. She disappeared as worm-filled earth tumbled down, extinguishing all the light in the world.

Brian's eyes snapped open, his scream interrupted by a spewing vomit of half-digested pizza and beer. He rolled over and coughed.

Brown cockroaches scurried across his body, some darting under the blanket while others huddled around a sliver of pepperoni stuck to his mattress.

Brian spit out a roach leg—one of the braver ones had crawled into his mouth—and slapped half-heartedly at the others, grimacing at the crunch of their chitinous bodies beneath his palm.

"I'm not dead yet, boys," he said to the roaches. "Happy fucking birthday to me."

The big four-oh, he thought. Over the hill and screaming toward the bottom at breakneck speed.

Brian swung his legs over the side of the bed and slowly stood up. He had a whopper of a hangover.

With his first step, he knocked over a half empty can of Miller High Life and warm beer squelched between his toes. Ten of its empty brothers, stacked into a pyramid of cans, stood next to a pizza box from Geno's Italian Eatery.

Brian rubbed his face and looked around his one-room efficiency on Chicago's south side. Pea-green paint that looked and smelled like the bottom of a diaper pail covered most of the walls, except for a dark stain above the sink that looked suspiciously like black mold. Water dripped from a corroded faucet on a mountain of dirty dishes.

His "fully furnished" apartment had one gate-leg table, four chairs, a twin bed, and a ratty couch in front of an ancient thirteen-inch television with a built-in VCR. The TV/VCR was actually bolted to a coffee table, as if someone would bother stealing it. The unit had come with an old-style pair of rabbit ears that picked up three and a half stations over the public airwaves on a good day.

That was before Brian had secretly connected the TV to the landlord's cable control box on the rooftop. A black coaxial cable snaked across the floor, up the wall, and out the window. It had been hell running the cable to the roof to mooch the signal, but it was the only way for Brian to watch and record the Chicago Bears.

Except for free cable, the place was a complete dump—but it was a step above the halfway house he'd been staying at since his release from prison. Well, maybe a half-step above was more accurate.

"Time to make the doughnuts," Brian said.

He stripped off his shirt, threw it on a pile of dirty clothes, and made his way over to the shower. When he turned the water on, a rust-colored stream gurgled out of the showerhead. Sighing, he glanced at the digital wall clock next to the sink. It glared accusingly at him, displaying 6:31 p.m.

Shit. He had less than an hour to shower and shave before reporting for the nightshift at Sweetum's Bakery. It was Brian's second job since getting out of prison. The first job had been bagging groceries at Food-For-Less, and he'd lost it a week ago when an asshole manager named Jake had discovered him taking home spoiled fruits and vegetables instead of throwing them in the dumpster.

Jake had threatened to call the cops but changed his mind after Brian shoved him against an alley wall and held a butterfly knife to the man's prodigious gut. The look on Jake's face had been one of utter surprise; obviously, he had not expected the mild-mannered Brian to go from zero to ape-shit in a split second.

Brian himself had been no less shocked. He'd never hurt anyone in his life, save for the time in prison when he'd stepped into the middle of a fight in the cafeteria. A hulking tattooed man with a shiv had slashed a young man from behind, thrown him to the floor, and was closing in for the kill.

Saving Tomas Tobias's life had cost Brian a shiv between his ribs and weeks in the hospital wing. It had cost the tattooed man his life.

After losing his job at Food-For-Less, Brian spent the next few days on the streets, scared shitless to return to the halfway house and find the cops on his doorstep. But the days passed, and no cops came. All the same, Brian gathered his few possessions in the dead of night and moved to his present shithole.

Brian stuck his hand under the shower and cursed. Still ice cold. He squirted a dollop of Barbasol into his palm and picked up a twin-bladed Bic that was ten shaves past its prime.

In the mirror, brown bloodshot eyes stared back at him from a fleshy face. Three years in prison had taken its toll on his mind, he knew that from the nightmares, but now he was starting to notice the effects on his body. His once thick black hair was ending up in the shower drain, while a layer of fat had accumulated around his midsection. His arms and legs were flabby, his flesh as white as a fish's belly. The changes had been so gradual over the span of three years that he hadn't really been aware of them.

Not only did he seem twenty pounds heavier, he could've sworn he was two inches shorter. Was it possible he'd gone from five-foot-ten to five-eight?

"How the fuck did you end up here?" Brian asked his reflection.

It had been a twisted trail from a happy home life to ex-con. Before his arrest, Brian would have described his life as perfect. He had a gorgeous wife, a faithful dog named Buster, and a modest home in a quiet suburban neighborhood west of Chicago. His job as a deliveryman for Schwartz's Office Emporium was nothing to write home about, but it paid the bills.

Cassidy couldn't have children of her own, but even that was no impediment to their happiness. The day after receiving this news from a fertility clinic, Brian opened a bank account to save money to adopt a baby. With this added expense, coupled with his mother-in-law's mounting medical bills, it was a struggle to make ends meet. But they were somehow making it work.

It was an average, by-the-book life he led, the proverbial American Dream of middle-class suburbia. Brian obeyed the speed limits, paid his taxes on time, and tried his best to live and let live. He didn't have much, but with Cassidy, Buster, and the hope of future children, it was more than enough.

Then one day, as Brian was making a delivery to a sketchy neighborhood not far from his present digs, he saw the flashing lights of a police cruiser in the rearview mirror.

Brian pulled over, worried he had a busted taillight. It would ruin his perfect driving record at Schwartz's of ten years without an accident or a traffic ticket. A perfect record meant a hefty Christmas bonus that sure would come in handy.

Brian rolled down the window.

"Hello, Officer. May I help you?"

The policeman's face was hidden behind reflective sunglasses that reminded Brian of the villain in *Terminator 2*. It made him nervous.

"Step out of the car, sir," said the officer.

"I've got my registration here somewhere," stammered Brian as he reached down and fumbled for his wallet.

"Keep your fucking hands where I can see them!"

Brian looked over to see a gun barrel inches from his face, and the entire world shrank down to the muzzle of a Glock 9mm pistol. He couldn't move.

"Hands on the steering wheel! Now!"

Brian tried to move his hands, but they wouldn't obey his brain's commands. The officer and his female partner yanked him out of his van, handcuffed him, read him his rights, and shoved him into the back of their cruiser.

Brian sat in a daze as he watched more cop cars arrive, including a K-9 unit. What the hell was going on? Why'd they stop him? He'd done nothing wrong. He was a good citizen, an honest taxpayer. Didn't they know he had rights?

A husky German shepherd jumped out of the K-9 unit and zeroed in on Brian's delivery van, its huge paws clawing at the doors excitedly. Brian winced at the fresh scratches running across Schwartz's Office Emporium.

Mr. Schwartz would be mad as hell when he saw that, Brian thought. His boss was a Chicago Alderman, a powerful member of the city council. Brian was sure Claude Schwartz would crack some skulls at CPD before the day was over.

Meanwhile, the cop with the mirrored sunglasses took out Brian's keys and opened the back of the van. The dog jumped inside, barking wildly at a box labeled *Printer Cartridges*. Another cop retrieved the box and sliced it open with a knife.

Plastic bags of what looked like marijuana spilled out. Lots of them. The dog danced around the bags like this was the best game in the world.

The next few days were a blur.

Brian was taken to a police station, fingerprinted, and booked on charges of resisting arrest and drug possession with intent to distribute. He made his phone call to Cassidy and was tossed into a communal holding cell with drunks, male prostitutes, and gangbangers.

Brian hotly proclaimed his innocence throughout the entire process, even as the cell door slammed shut. His fellow inmates jeered and ribbed each other at his protests.

"We're all innocent, asshole," said one.

"Yeah, I was framed," said another.

"Fucking cops planted my DNA," said a third. "Same as they did for OJ."

Brian picked the edge of a bench, well away from everyone, and sat down to wait.

One cross-dresser in black stockings, who introduced himself as Roxanne (and did so with a straight face), sat beside him. Except for the prominent Adam's apple, it would've been difficult to tell if Roxanne was a man or a woman. Either way, there were hard lessons etched in the lines of his face.

After a time, Brian told Roxanne about the day's events. The man sat with crossed legs, sometimes asking a question or having him repeat something.

"I don't belong here," finished Brian. "There's been some mistake."

Roxanne patted his shoulder. "I believe you."

"You do?"

Roxanne nodded sagely. "Spend enough time in these places, you get to where you can spot the ones who belong and the ones who don't. You were in the wrong place at the wrong time. Or you're someone's patsy."

"A fall guy?"

"Right," said Roxanne. "If that's the case, you'd better figure out who put the finger on you, or you're going to do hard time."

"I'm innocent. Doesn't that count for something?"

Roxanne laughed. "You'd think that, right? But that doesn't mean shit. If you're rich, you hire slick lawyers or bribe your way to freedom. If you're poor, the wheels of justice grind you up and spit you out."

"If you're looking for something to spit out, faggot," said a tattooed biker, "I've got something for you." The biker made an obscene gesture with his crotch.

"In your dreams, sweetheart," Roxanne spat back. "Besides, I'd have to find it first."

The other inmates laughed, but the biker's eyes smoldered. "Watch your back, faggot. One day you'll find me behind you, and I'll give you a red smile from ear to ear." He made a slashing motion across his throat.

Roxanne laughed again. "I'm not impressed, bitch." He held up his right bicep and flexed it. Brian caught a glimpse of a small tattoo, a symbol he did not recognize. The other prisoners, including the biker, fell silent and edged away from Roxanne, as if the tattoo were some magical talisman.

Brian kept his questions to himself.

Hours passed. Brian was on the verge of falling asleep on the bench when a cop called out his name. "Brian Piccolo. Your wife is here with a public defender."

"Good luck," said Roxanne.

Brian said goodbye and followed the cop to a small, windowless room. Inside, he found his wife Cassidy talking with a tall, good-looking man dressed in an expensive black suit.

"Lance Kincaid," said the man. His handshake was iron. "Have a seat."

At first, Brian couldn't believe his luck. Kincaid was no run-of-the-mill public defender, but an associate at a high-powered law firm in downtown Chicago.

Part of his duties at Larson & Goldfarb, explained the attorney, was to do *pro bono* work for people who might not have the means to hire an attorney.

"This representation is completely free," said Kincaid with a smile.

"Aren't we lucky?" exclaimed Cassidy. "A real attorney is going to defend you! One of the best in the city."

Brian was elated, but he did not like the way Kincaid's eyes roved over Cassidy when he thought no one was looking, or how closely he sat next to her. Cassidy was a beautiful redhead, ten years younger than Brian, who drew stares wherever she went. He thanked his lucky stars that she was absolutely devoted to him.

"Before we talk about today's events," began Kincaid, "let's get to know one another. For starters, are you any relation to the Brian Piccolo, running back for the Chicago Bears who died of cancer in 1969?"

Brian shook his head. "That Brian Piccolo passed away in 1970. I'm named after him, though. My father was a huge Bears fan, just like his father before him. He cried like a baby when he watched *Brian's Song* on TV. When I came along in 1978, he named me Brian."

"Too bad," said Kincaid. "Being related to a local sports icon would score huge points with a jury." He turned to Cassidy with a dazzling smile. "How'd you two meet?"

Brian didn't like the question. It was code for, "How did a guy like this score a knockout like you?" But he said nothing.

"Do you want to tell him?" asked Cassidy.

"You tell it," said Brian.

"Okay. I was taking my puppy for a walk in our favorite park. Somehow, Buster slipped his leash and ran into a busy street. He was so fast I couldn't catch him, and I could only watch as a huge truck barreled toward him. Out of the blue, a stranger raced into the street, snatched Buster off the pavement, and dove for the sidewalk. The truck never even stopped. A year later, Brian and I were married."

"What a story!" said Kincaid. Brian couldn't tell if the man's voice was tinged with admiration or mocking incredulity. "You wouldn't catch a selfish bastard like me risking my neck for a dog. You're the better man, Brian."

"Then why am I on this side of the table?"

"Let's talk about that," said Kincaid. "Start with what you were doing before the arrest. Leave nothing out, no matter how trivial it might seem."

For the second time, Brian unfolded the day's events. Kincaid listened attentively, took notes, and asked questions whenever something was unclear. When Brian got to the part about the drug-sniffing dog scratching through the *Schwartz* in Schwartz's Office Emporium, Kincaid help up a hand.

"Hold it. Your boss is Claude Schwartz, the Alderman?" asked Kincaid.

"Yes."

Alarm flashed in Kincaid's eyes, a shooting star briefly disturbing a calm sky.

"Is that significant?" asked Brian.

Kincaid cleared his throat, his mask of professionalism firmly in place once more. "Not especially. Please continue."

When their time was up, Kincaid admonished Brian not to answer any questions without him present, then offered to drive Cassidy home.

Cassidy politely refused but gave in after Brian said it would be safer than taking the bus and walking through Chicago at night.

Afterwards, Brian was transferred to a smaller cell with two bunks. Perched in the top bunk, eyeing him curiously, was Roxanne.

"Hello, Brian Piccolo."

"Hey, Roxanne."

Brian took the bottom bunk and lay down. He was so very

tired.

Roxanne's face appeared from the edge of the top bunk. "That's not my real name, as you may have guessed. It's my favorite song by my favorite band. My real name is Tomas Tobias."

"So...you're not a prostitute?"

Tomas laughed, a musical sound incongruous to the gun-metal gray cell walls. Brian decided he liked Tomas, even if he was a criminal.

"I'm many things," said Tomas, "but I'm not a prostitute. No, my many partners are completely free and consensual. The police were raiding a particular downtown establishment and found a little weed in my purse. Here I am."

"Then what are you?" asked Brian.

The younger man lowered his voice. "I'm a fixer."

Brian didn't understand. "A fixer?"

"I fix complex problems for an exclusive clientele." He made a shooting gesture with his forefinger and thumb, and Brian again saw the tattoo on his right arm. "No matter who, no matter where."

"Tomas?"

"Yeah?"

"Shut up and go to sleep. Just don't kill me, please."

A week went by. At Brian and Cassidy's next meeting with Lance Kincaid, Brian could see from the attorney's face that something was wrong.

Somehow, said Kincaid, Brian's fingerprints were found on several of the marijuana bags from the delivery van. Since the amount of drugs seized was over 5,000 grams, a Class 1 Felony, Brian faced four to fifteen years in state prison and a fine of up to $25,000, or both.

With Brian's prints on the bags, Kincaid explained, the case was a slam-dunk for the prosecution. Even so, the attorney had convinced the prosecutor handling the case to cut a deal: three years and no fine, if Brian pled guilty.

"But I'm innocent!" Brian exclaimed. "I had no idea the

drugs were even back there. And I never touched those bags, I swear to God. You believe me, don't you?"

"Of course," said Cassidy.

"Sure, sure," said Kincaid. "But if we go to trial, the prosecution is going to kill us with the physical evidence. Believe me, you don't want a jury to decide this. They'll be pissed that they're missing work or their soap operas or whatever to deal with a man who, in their minds, is obviously guilty. You'll go to jail, possibly for fifteen years."

"Take the deal," pleaded Cassidy.

"Your wife's right."

"But I'm innocent, Mr. Kincaid."

"It's not about guilt or innocence," said the attorney. "It's about whether you can create reasonable doubt in a juror's mind. It's about whether or not you can win. You can't win."

"Listen to Lance," said Cassidy.

The familiarity in his wife's voice made Brian scowl. When had she started calling Mr. Kincaid by his first name?

"There's one more thing," said Kincaid. "You'll have to sign a confession that you and you alone were selling the drugs."

Brian's scowl deepened. "Is that normal?"

"That's the deal," said Kincaid. "I suggest you take it, while it's still on the table."

"Three years isn't that long," said Cassidy. "Buster and I will still be home, waiting for you."

The cheap Bic razor cut into Brian's face.

"Liar," said Brian. He dabbed at his bloody neck with toilet paper. "Three years? You didn't even wait six months before filing for divorce."

Brian splashed tepid water on his face and selected the least dirty towel to dry himself. He turned off the shower.

Fuck it, thought Brian. Fuck the job and fuck everything.

He glanced over to the window. Outside, evening was settling on this neighborhood of graffitied buildings with broken windows, of poor kids playing in the streets, of older kids selling drugs or boosting cars. Occasionally, gunfire sounded in the distance like the pop of firecrackers.

Brian went over to the window and looked down to the street. Five stories up. Was that high enough? Or would he end up in the emergency room with medical bills he could never afford to pay?

He opened the window and let in an inviting breeze. What if he took a swan dive, head-first, straight down to the concrete sidewalk? That would surely do it.

Why not?

Brian stuck his head out of the window and put one foot on the windowsill, but the sounds of a familiar song stopped him. He spun around to see what had made the sound, banging his head on the bottom of the window.

It was the *Monday Night Football* theme song. The TV/VCR had turned itself on to record the Bears game. Who were they playing?

Brian closed the window and rubbed his head. "After the game," he told it. "I'll watch one more game."

He grabbed two cans of Miller High Life from the fridge, picked up a slice of pizza from this morning's pizza box, and sat down on the couch.

"Dear God, this is Brian Paul Piccolo," he said to the ceiling. "My life has turned to shit. I want it to be over, but I don't want to go to hell for suicide. Are you there?"

No answer.

"If the Bears win tonight, I won't go through with it. But if they lose, that's it. I'm punching my ticket. Amen."

"Tonight," said an announcer, "the oh-and-one Bears face a tough matchup against quarterback Russell Wilson and the vaunted Legion of Boom defense of the Seattle Seahawks."

"Aw, fuck," said Brian. "Well, a deal's a deal. I'm a man of my word."

He turned up the volume, opened one of the beers (setting the other aside for his absent father), and watched the game of his life.

With 1:11 left in the second quarter of the game, Brian was starting to like his odds of surviving the night. The Bears had just kicked a field goal and had so far shut out the Seahawks, leading 10-0. The Bears' defense, with the addition of outside linebacker Khalil Mack from the Raiders, looked incredibly stout. They should be, thought Brian, considering the fact the Bears had given up two first round picks in the trade.

The game went to a commercial break.

Brian downed the last of his Miller High Life, crumpled the can in one hand, and tossed it over his shoulder. He picked up the beer he'd set out for his father.

"Here's to you, Pops," he said, and cracked open the Champagne of Beers. It was Brian's tradition to always leave a beer out for his father during the game, then drink it in Jim Piccolo's memory.

Jim was a Chicago native, a dyed-in-the-wool Bears fan who remembered the days before the Super Bowl era, when the original Monsters of the Midway terrorized the NFL. Brian had heard his dad wax poetic about the 1940 NFL Championship Game, when the Bears crushed the Washington Redskins 73-0.

"*That* team was the greatest Bears team," Jim would tell his son. "Not the eighty-five Bears." It was a friendly debate between them that went on for over thirty years, until Jim Piccolo's heart attack.

Brian disagreed. Ditka's '85 Bears would dance the Super Bowl Shuffle right over the 1940 team, exactly like they did to eighteen other teams en route to winning Super Bowl XX.

The commercials were over, and the Seahawks had the ball with more than a minute until the end of the half. Surely the Bears could keep the shutout going?

But no. Russell Wilson moved the ball down the field with calm precision, and Seattle kicked a field goal to make the halftime score 10-3.

"Predictable," said Brian.

Seattle was a good team, a perennial playoff contender with Wilson at quarterback. What had the Bears done recently? Four straight years as the cellar-dwellers in the NFC North. Why would this year be any different?

Brian's hopes improved—slightly—when the Bears were up 17-3 in the fourth quarter with 14:15 left to play. But Brian knew that was an eternity in football, and no lead was safe against a talented quarterback like Wilson. As Brian expected, Seattle rallied, shaving the margin to 17-10 with Wilson's deep touchdown pass to Tyler Lockett. The Bears couldn't answer and were forced to punt. Once again, Seattle had the ball and was moving down the field. Even though the Bears were leading, defeat seemed certain.

"Here it comes, Pops," said Brian. "This is where we let another fourth-quarter lead slip away. Wilson will tie the game, then win it in overtime."

Brian wondered if it would hurt much when his head smacked the pavement. Surely the pain would be momentary?

But then, a miracle happened. Wilson dropped back to pass, then fired a quick throw to the left flat. Prince Amukamara, cornerback for the Bears, jumped the route and intercepted the ball, returning it all the way for a touchdown.

"*Pick-Six!*" yelled Brian. "*Touchdown, Bears!*" The beer can flew from his hands as he leaped off the couch and started dancing the Super Bowl Shuffle, doing his best imitation of the legendary Walter Payton. "Thank you, God."

It wasn't so much his life that Brian was thankful for. Not really. What was his life worth, without Cass and Buster? No, he was thankful for the Bears' victory, and the hope of more victories to come. If they could beat Seattle, they could beat anyone. It wasn't much to live for, but it was something.

On the television, the camera was panning the crowd, getting their reaction to the touchdown. These were the shots Brian enjoyed the most, the ones featuring cute babies dressed entirely in Bears regalia, fat guys high fiving each other, or attractive ladies screaming with delight.

The camera operator had found a particularly striking redheaded woman in a luxury booth. She was jumping up and down excitedly, pumping her fists, while the man next to her texted on his phone, obviously bored.

Brian froze mid-shuffle. "Cass?" He fumbled for the remote, rewound the recording, and then pressed playback in slow motion.

It *was* Cassidy…and the man with his face in the cell phone was his former attorney, Lance Kincaid. There were more people in the luxury booth, all well-dressed, including another familiar face sitting next to Kincaid.

Brian paused the image.

"Claude Schwartz," said Brian. His former boss, the owner of Schwartz's Office Emporium and Chicago Alderman.

Brian sat down heavily on the couch. He did not move or speak for a long time. When the game was over, Brian reached into his pocket, took out a flip-phone, and punched in a number.

"Tomas? It's Brian Piccolo. Yeah, I saw the game. Listen, I'm calling in that favor you promised me. There's someone I need to kill."

December 14, 2018, 7:04 p.m.
Lincoln Park, Chicago

Lance Kincaid straightened his reflection's tie, a Viola Milano handmade in Italy. It was a deep red with a pattern of green swirls—the catalog had described it as "merlot and emerald"—but in Lance's mind it was dried blood on blades of grass, the colors one might see on the savanna after a lion's kill.

The color scheme was an excellent choice for an up-and-coming associate at Larson & Goldfarb, one of Chicago's most prestigious law firms. Red bespoke courage, aggression, and power, while the green softened it just enough not to be threatening to his superiors. Solid ties, or ties with bold colors, were the province of senior partners.

"One day soon, Old Sport," he said aloud. He combed his brown hair—close-cropped on the sides, wavy on top. Kincaid was a tall man, made taller by the special insoles he secretly wore, bluff-faced and barrel-chested, with large, grasping hands calloused from weightlifting rather than manual labor. Despite long hours in his office or a courtroom, his skin had the healthy glow of a man who spent time outdoors. That, at least, came naturally, from jogging through downtown Chicago or the trails crisscrossing the exclusive gated community he lived in.

Kincaid put down his comb and grinned, white teeth shining in a devilish mouth. "Old Sport, you're gonna knock 'em dead tonight."

He called himself Old Sport not because anyone had given him the nickname, but because he remembered the phrase from some old book he'd read in high school. He didn't remember the title, but that wasn't important. He preferred Old Sport to the nickname started by his fraternity brothers at Pi Kappa Alpha—The Chameleon.

In college: "Boys, The Chameleon passed for twenty-one.

135

Scored beer for the kegger!" "The Chameleon talked a virgin's clothes right off. Her legs were spread for everyone before the night was done."

In law school: "Georgetown didn't stand a chance against The Chameleon in moot court." "The Chameleon's been offered five—count 'em, five—summer internships!"

At trial: "The Chameleon talked a jury out of convicting Alderman Schwartz of campaign fraud." "Treble damages for patent infringement. The Chameleon strikes again!"

Could Kincaid help it if he had the God-given ability to blend in, to adapt himself, to any situation? It had gotten him laid countless times and won him an impressive number of jury trials. Was the girl a democratic socialist? He could bemoan the evils of capitalism with the best of them. Was she a lover of modern art? He could bullshit about Fauvism or post-modern narratives hidden in squiggly lines.

At trial, did he need to be kind and fatherly, garnering sympathy for an otherwise unsympathetic client like Alderman Schwartz? Or did he need to deliver a fiery speech of righteous indignation, to make a jury of average men and women care that one rich company infringed the intellectual property of another? He could do both with ease.

Whatever the Chameleon was, he was an expert liar.

Tonight, for his law firm's Holiday Mixer, Kincaid's role was associate bucking for partner, and it was a subtle one: be confident but not haughty, be friendly but not overly familiar, and kiss the asses of the senior partners without being obsequious or servile.

Like everything, it started with first impressions, and that began with one's wardrobe. For the *coup de grace* to his ensemble, Kincaid fastened his gold-plated Swiss Jaeger-LeCoultre watch, positioning it to where it was just visible beneath the cuff of his black Brioni suit. There! He was ready for battle.

"Knock who dead?" said a voice from the bedroom.

"The firm's partnership committee," said Kincaid, carefully

not mentioning Penelope Lambert by name. "There are two spots open since Sam Lively croaked and Petra Rodgers retired. I'm up for nomination at the end of the year, remember?"

A redheaded woman a few years younger than Kincaid's thirty-two stepped into the bathroom, balanced on high heels beneath a layered chiffon dress with a long skirt. The first word to describe Cassidy Piccolo Kincaid was usually gorgeous, often modified by drop-dead. Kincaid was a tits-man, and always had been, but Cassidy's long, muscular legs had gone a long way to converting him into a legs-man. Her green eyes shone with a light that was simultaneously gentle and strong.

"Nice tie," said Cassidy. She came over to her husband of six months and straightened it. "Red and green for Christmas, perfect for your firm's Christmas party."

Kincaid frowned. "You think this is a Christmas tie?"

"Sure. It's festive."

"Festive? Aw, shit." Kincaid unslung the tie and brushed past his wife to the master bedroom. He threw open a closet and rummaged through a tie rack. "I have to find something else to wear."

Cassidy followed him, concern on her face. "Honey, what's wrong? We need to get going, or we're going to be late."

"I can't wear a Christmas tie!" he hissed.

A Labrador retriever, disturbed from his nap, looked up from his bed in a corner of the room. His ears were pricked attentively.

"Why not?"

"It's not a fucking Christmas party for starters," said Kincaid. "It's a Holiday Mixer. Half of our partners are Jewish, and the other half don't celebrate Christmas beyond giving gifts. So, you'd better not say, 'Merry Christmas,' to anybody."

The dog was up now. He trotted over to Cassidy and stood at her feet, his body weight rolled forward, his tail lifted, and his mouth shut. His attention was focused on Kincaid.

Cassidy put a hand on the dog's head, but he did not relax. "Easy, Buster." She turned to Kincaid. "I don't like saying 'happy holidays.' It sounds so antiseptic."

Kincaid shot her a venomous look, one he sometimes wore if he'd had a surprise witness or an unfavorable ruling from a judge. Their short time as husband and wife had been happy, but Cassidy already knew to keep herself and Buster away from Lance when he was in one of his moods.

He was definitely in one tonight.

"These are your people, and you know what's best," Cassidy relented. "Buster, go back to bed."

The dog obeyed, but kept his eyes trained on Kincaid.

"That's my girl," said Kincaid. He pulled out a blue tie swirled with yellow. "How's this?"

"Too drab. Here, try this one." Cassidy selected a burgundy-and-silver tie. "Confident, but not over-powering."

Kincaid nodded. "Good choice, babe. How do I look?"

"Fabulous." She bent forward to kiss him, but Kincaid stepped back.

"Don't get lipstick on me." He looked his wife up and down, his face pinched into a frown. "Baby, this isn't the dress I picked out for you. Where's the black one?"

"Don't you like this one?"

"It's fine if you're north of fifty and get your kicks playing bingo at church."

Kincaid went into her closet and returned with a black dress. It was strapless, with a plunging neckline and a slit in the skirt that ran up to mid-thigh.

"I want everyone to see how gorgeous my new bride is," said Kincaid. He held out the dress.

"It's cold outside."

"You'll be warm enough under your mink stole."

"I don't like real fur," said Cassidy petulantly. "Fur hurts."

Kincaid rolled his eyes. "I didn't see you objecting to your fillet mignon yesterday. And how many pairs of leather shoes do you own? And when you drive your Beamer to your tennis lessons, what's cradling that gorgeous ass of yours? Yes, genuine leather from a dead animal. So, don't give me any bullshit about fur hurts. Every fucking thing hurts."

"You win, counselor," said Cassidy. "You always do." She snatched the dress from him and began stripping.

"Damn straight I win." Kincaid sat in a chair and watched her change, drinking her in, and thought about the first time they'd met.

It was during a *pro bono* consultation for her ex-husband, a delivery driver accused of selling drugs from his van. Kincaid, like most big law attorneys, despised *pro bono* work. How did the partners expect associates to bill insane hours while "giving back to the less fortunate" in the community?

Kincaid had become a corporate attorney, so he didn't have to deal with the lowlifes and the criminals. If a woman got slapped around a little, so what? She was probably mouthing off, and what woman didn't like for her man to get a little rough before sex? As for those accused of crimes, most of them were guilty as sin. And if they were stupid enough to get caught, they deserved to go to jail. (Unless they could afford the firm's exorbitant fees, of course.)

Kincaid's standard approach to *pro bono* work was to dash off temporary restraining orders for the domestic violence victims and advise accused criminals to take a plea, no matter the merits of the case.

It was a lucky thing getting assigned to Piccolo's case. Not only did Kincaid get to do a solid for one of the firm's best clients, he met Cassidy.

At some point during the initial consultation, with Piccolo rambling on about being framed, Kincaid had fallen hopelessly in love with the man's wife—in other words, he was seized by an overpowering desire to possess her.

When Piccolo followed Kincaid's advice and took a plea, the man left a lonely and grief-stricken wife with a hefty mortgage, a sick mother going through chemotherapy, and a stack of medical bills a mile high.

The Chameleon set to work.

At first, Cassidy was resolved to faithfully wait three years for her husband's release. She believed Brian's story that he was an innocent man caught by dreadful circumstances, and Kincaid came to realize she would continue to wait as long as this belief persisted.

So, the attorney assumed the roles of friend and confidant to disabuse Cassidy of this notion. One evening over coffee (dropping by to check in on her), Kincaid told Cassidy that Brian himself had secretly confessed his guilt.

It was a lie, of course. But he told it so well, with such conviction, that she never questioned it. She cried bitter tears, and Kincaid offered a comforting shoulder.

"Cassidy, I know this has been difficult to hear," Kincaid said, "but Brian knew his delivery van was filled with drugs."

"Why would he do something so stupid?" she sobbed. "We had our whole lives ahead of us."

Kincaid edged closer. A yellow Labrador, curled under Cassidy's feet, growled in his throat. He eyed Kincaid's ankle as if it were a strange cat.

"Brian wanted to give you the life you deserved, Cassidy. That's what he said. Delivering drugs to neighborhoods on the South Side seemed the easiest way to do that."

"I can hardly believe it."

"Believe it." He laid a hand on her arm. "The sooner you accept that, the sooner you can get on with your life."

Her eyes blazed at his last remark, and Kincaid realized he'd overstepped himself. He switched gears smoothly. "It's admirable that you want to wait for Brian. I mean it. Not many women in your position would wait for a convicted felon. Three years is a long time, but you can do it."

Kincaid read the changes in Cassidy's face as she began to associate "convicted felon" and "liar" with her conception of Brian.

There were more visits, more coffees, and more tears. Cassidy filed for divorce six months after the arrest. Two years later, Cassidy Piccolo became Cassidy Kincaid.

After their honeymoon, Kincaid went about paying off all of her outstanding debt, including her mother's medical bills. (Thankfully, the old bat had croaked soon after the wedding. She always seemed to see right through him.)

Kincaid whisked Cassidy away from a life on the edge of poverty and gave her the finest of everything. He sold her house, traded in her decrepit Ford Escort for a Beamer, and threw out all reminders of Brian Piccolo.

The only thing that remained of her old life was that stupid dog. How long did the average Labrador live, anyway?

"How do I look, Lance?"

Kincaid didn't answer his wife.

"Honey? How do I look in this dress?"

The vision of Cassidy in her black dress snapped Kincaid back to the present like a rubber band. His eyes started at her high heels, ran up the smooth legs, and ended with the freckles along the tops of her breasts. He got no higher than that.

"You look fine. Better than fine, in fact."

Kincaid stood up. There was a noticeable bulge in his pants.

"Lance," said Cassidy with exasperation, "we're going to be late. We don't have time to get undressed and dressed again."

"Who said anything about getting undressed?" Kincaid unzipped his pants, dropped his boxers, and sat down on the edge of the bed. He looked at her expectantly.

"Not now."

"Come on, babe. It will help me relax."

Sighing heavily, Cassidy came over, got on her knees, and put her face between his legs.

"Catch all of it," said Kincaid. "I don't want any stains on my Brioni."

December 14, 2018, 9:55 p.m.
Wicker Park, Chicago

"There's the taco truck," said Tomas to Brian. "Exactly where I said it would be."

Tomas pulled his Jeep Wrangler to the side of the street and killed the engine. Brian sat in the passenger's seat, eyes on the truck, barely breathing. This was it, the final piece to the puzzle. After months of planning with Tomas, he'd have his weapon. On Sunday, he'd walk out of Soldier Stadium, scot-free and no one the wiser.

The taco truck was parked with three other food trucks in a cul-de-sac next to a nice apartment building. The steam coming off the truck's roof gave it a particularly demonic look, despite being festooned in Christmas lights.

Next to the food trucks, customers huddled in small groups beneath heat lamps, their faces buried in expensive phones. It was a young crowd of mostly Caucasians. The neighborhood of Wicker Park was a hipster haven, with its copious vintage boutiques, vegetarian restaurants, and artisanal food trucks.

To Brian, it hardly seemed the place to buy an untraceable gun. But then, what did he know about the workings of Chicago's criminal underworld? That was Tomas's department.

Brian was about to open the passenger door, but Tomas put a hand on his arm. The younger man's hands were smooth and hairless, almost feminine. They didn't look like the hands of a killer.

"Not so fast, Bri. It's not after ten yet."

"Does that really matter?"

"Absolutely." Tomas ran delicate fingers through his wavy black hair, a nervous habit. He wore a leather Chicago Bulls jacket, white T-shirt, and jeans. Without his makeup and his Roxanne garb, he could pass for an average college kid. "You have to do this exactly as I told you, or no gun. Let's go over it again."

"I'm listening."

Tomas ticked off points on his fingers. "Ask for Jesse, first thing. Say you want the Number Five Burrito Special. And don't forget to ask for extra sour cream."

"Got it," said Brian. "Ask for Jesse. Order the Number Five Burrito Special with extra sour cream. Anything else?"

"Yes." Tomas fished out his wallet and handed Brian a wad of bills. The outside bills were fivers, in case any other customers were around. "Hand Jesse the cash and say, 'Keep the change.'"

Brian took the cash and stuffed it in his pocket. He eyed the makeshift food court and the four trucks. Despite the lateness of the hour, the crowd was growing. "Shouldn't we wait for the customers to clear? There's so many people around."

"Don't worry about it," said Tomas. "Jesse is a pro's pro. I've seen her pass out the special even when cops are in line."

"No shit?"

"Would I shit a shitter?"

Brian exhaled heavily. "It's now or never, Tommy." He started to open the door, and once again Tomas laid a hand on Brian's shoulder.

"Let me take care of this, my friend. Say the word, and it's done."

"Tommy, we talked about this."

"I'm going to retire from the business soon. You can come with me. We'll live out of our suitcases, go where the winds take us."

Brian sighed. "You know I don't swing that way, Tommy. If I did, you'd be at the top of the list."

"The top? No fooling?"

"The very top. Like a cherry."

Tomas laughed, but it was half-hearted. "You're not like me, Bri. You're not a cold-blooded killer."

Brian shrugged him off. "Tell that to Big Danny Cowher. I

took a shiv for you, Tommy. Right between the ribs, inches from my heart, but that didn't stop me from crushing Cowher's windpipe. If I can face him, I can do this."

Tomas's eyes were cloudy with the memory of the day Brian saved his life in the prison cafeteria. "I'm forever grateful for what you did. You acted bravely, without a thought for your own safety, like when you saved that dog you told me about."

"Buster," said Brian. Sometimes, he missed his dog even more than he did Cassidy. Was that wrong?

"It's different when you're face to face with a person," said Tomas. "When you look into their eyes, and you know that they know you're going to kill them. It's a moment you'll never forget."

"That's the whole point, Tommy. I want to see that look. I want him to know it was me. Look, I appreciate all you've done to pull off the perfect murder."

"The planning part is always easy. The execution is something else."

"Are you kidding?" asked Brian. "Getting me a job at Soldier Field was easy? Finding Rico was easy?"

"Rico was a stroke of genius," admitted Tomas, "even if I do say so myself." He glanced at his watch. "It's after ten now. You're on."

Brian exited the Jeep and walked slowly over to the taco truck. The customers along the way hardly gave him a second glance. They texted on phones, ate their food, or smoked cigarettes. Some were engrossed in a board game with complex pieces whose object Brian could not even begin to guess. These were people who lived in a different Chicago, one that was relatively safe. You could go out at night here, without fear of getting robbed or shot.

The hipsters were a strange bunch, most of them transplants from other states like California. Not one of them sported a Bears, Cubs, or Bulls scarf or jacket, as one might expect to find on a cold December night. Instead, Brian saw the names of teams he did not recognize. Who the hell were the Arsenal?

"Old-timer," said one as Brian passed. He had a patchy beard and what looked like a French beret perched jauntily atop a mop of greasy hair. He wasn't much younger than Brian.

"Hey, Old-timer! You wanna play some Catan?"

Brian glanced around before realizing the man was talking to him. "You talking to me?"

Beard-o nodded. "Tess here has to bow out of the game. You wanna take her place?"

Brian politely refused.

"Your loss," said Beard-o. "She's winning."

"Thanks for the offer," said Brian. He moved away from the group, trying his best to keep his face out of the light from the heat lamps.

Brian stepped into line. The girl in front of him was wrapped in a huge pink scarf that read: *I'm with her.* She ordered Baja shrimp tacos, mango salsa, and a Mexican Coke in a squeaky voice that sounded like an over chewed dog's toy.

The woman working the window had dark hair and a friendly smile that showed off her perfect white teeth. On her nametag was written *Hi, I'm Jesse! Ask about our specials!* in flowing cursive.

The girl with the scarf moved off, and Brian was at the front of the line. He stood there for some moments, unable to remember what he was supposed to say.

Jesse smiled down at him. "Too many choices?"

Brian found his voice. "Are you Jesse?"

"So says my nametag and my mother. What'll it be, sir?"

"I'd like the Number Five Burrito Special."

Surprise flickered across Jesse's face. "We only have four specials. I think you're mistaken."

Panic welled up in Brian's throat. Mistaken? She was supposed to take his order, no questions asked. Had he made a mistake?

"I have other customers behind you," said Jesse. "Order

something off the menu, or step aside."

Then Brian remembered. "I'll have the Number Five Burrito Special, with extra sour cream." He handed over the cash with the two fivers displayed on either side. "Keep the change."

Jesse looked him up and down, nodding to herself. "I'll see what Paco can whip up. Can I have a name?"

Brian almost gave his real name but changed it mid-word. "Bradley."

"Step to the side, Bradly. It'll be right out."

Brian waited for his order, shivering in the cold. After a few minutes, Jesse returned to the window and called for Bradley.

Brian stood there, blinking.

"Bradley? Your order is ready."

"Oh!" Brian stepped forward and took two sacks. The first sack was light and smelled delicious. The second one was much heavier.

"Thanks."

"Come again," said Jesse. "Next, please."

Brian walked off, fighting the urge to peek into the second bag. What if the gun clattered to the ground, right in front of all these people, many of whom had probably never seen a real gun? Would they run? Crawl into fetal positions? Call the cops?

Brian walked briskly back to the Jeep and got inside.

"Don't open the bag," said Tomas as he started the engine. "Give it to me."

Brian did as he was told, though he was dying to see what was inside. Tomas took the bag, opened a small compartment in his floorboard (one which Brian had never seen nor suspected was there), and dropped the bag inside.

"Open the other bag," said Tomas. "I'm starving."

Brian handed his friend one of two burritos. Brian took a bite, surprised to find a complex interplay of spices dancing on his palate. "This is fantastic, Tommy."

"Jesse wants to go straight and open a restaurant," said Tomas between mouthfuls. "Everyone has a dream, right?" He drove through the city, carefully obeying every traffic signal along the way. Eventually, he pulled into a private parking garage, gave a hand signal to the attendant on duty, and drove to a spot marked *Reserved—Tommy Boy*.

When Tomas parked the car, he pulled the bag from the secret compartment. "This is a private garage, one owned entirely by the people I work for. Now, let's take a look at the Number Five Burrito Special."

"With extra sour cream," threw in Brian. "I almost forgot that part."

Tomas put on latex gloves to keep his fingerprints off the contents of the bag, and he made Brian do the same. Then he reached in and brought out three wrapped bundles. The largest contained a sleek black handgun. The other two were a suppressor and a magazine loaded with ten hollow-point rounds.

Tomas whistled softly as he held up the gun for inspection. The dark weapon seemed to drink the light and swallow it whole. He twisted it in the air, nodding in approval.

"This is a real beauty," said Tomas.

"What is it?" To Brian's untrained eye, it was an ordinary-looking black pistol. It reminded him of a smaller version of the gun carried by Bruce Willis in *Die Hard*.

"This, my friend, is the 9mm Beretta M9A3 semiautomatic pistol with a threaded barrel. Professional grade. Originally designed for the U.S. Army, though they eventually went with a Sig Sauer. Big mistake, in my opinion."

"Seems like an awfully nice gun to use once and throw away," said Brian.

"If you were in the business, like me, you wouldn't think so. But you're a civilian, so to you, this gun is what we call a burner. A one-and-done gun."

"Do I throw out the silencer, too?" Brian held up a cylindrical piece of metal.

Tomas groaned. "That's a suppressor, and the answer is yes. When you're done, you pick up the ejected casings and you give the gun, suppressor, magazine, and unused rounds to me for proper disposal."

"Right. And this is the magazine?" asked Brian as he held up the mechanism.

"Holy shit. What do you know about guns?"

"You shoot bad guys with the pointy end," said Brian, attempting levity.

Tomas was not amused. "This isn't *Game of Thrones*," he said, catching the reference. "It's one of the world's most efficient machines designed specifically to kill humans. The suppressor screws into the 'pointy end.'"

"The barrel," said Brian. "I know what it's called."

"Good for you," said Tomas. "The magazine you're holding is loaded with ten hollow-point rounds. Do you know the significance of firing hollow points versus conventional rounds?"

"I'm about to find out, right?"

Tomas nodded. "The hollow point at the tip of the bullet increases tissue damage along the path of the wound. It does so because the pressure created in the pit allows the bullet to expand, opening up like a mushroom in the body. The fragments are less likely to leave the target and strike something behind, which is good for our purposes. If we're lucky, there will be no fragments left behind for forensics."

"So hollow points are deadlier than regular bullets."

"Correct." Tomas put the gun back in the bag, along with the suppressor and the magazine. "The lesson is over for the day. Tomorrow, we'll go to a private gun range."

"Target practice!" said Brian enthusiastically.

"You aren't shooting anything," said Tomas. "Not until you learn the basics of gun safety. By this time tomorrow, you'll know everything you need to know about this gun."

December 14, 2018, 10:15 p.m.
The Loop, Chicago

"Merrry Chrissstmas, Lance!" slurred Claude Schwartz. He pumped Lance's hand vigorously and turned to Cassidy. "And a very merry Christmas to you, gorgeous." Schwartz, a middle-aged bear of a man with a curly white beard, encircled her in his burly arms, lifted her off the floor, and kissed her cheek.

Cassidy coughed into her hand as he set her down. Schwartz reeked of booze and cigar smoke.

"Merry Christmas," returned Lance smoothly. He looked at Cassidy.

"Happy holidays, Mr. Schwartz," she said.

Cassidy felt the heat of Lance's glare. Apparently, she had said the wrong thing. Again. Far from being a relaxing evening, the Larson & Goldfarb Holiday Mixer was turning out to be an utterly exhausting experience.

Her husband's colleagues were either complete lushes, many of them as plastered as Schwartz, or two-faced backbiters who judged everyone and everything. One and all, they fawned over the senior partners, and they were all dressed to the nines.

For a secularized Holiday Mixer, Christmas trees with giant wrapped gifts beneath them were everywhere, fully decorated and lit up like Times Square. Waiters in black tails circled the revelers with drinks and hors d'oeuvres, while a jazz pianist crooned holiday tunes.

Cassidy knew she didn't belong here, with these people. They were highly educated, extremely opinionated, overworked alphas. She was a junior college dropout from a middle-class family, a girl who preferred beer and pretzels to champagne and caviar.

Not for the first time, Cassidy wished she were home with her dog Buster, watching predictable Hallmark Christmas movies while curled up on the sofa. In these reveries, she was with Brian, not Lance, on the tattered green sofa in their drafty old house.

Poor Brian was out of prison by now, but she had no idea where he was or what he was doing. It was just as well. He'd turned out to be a liar and a drug-dealer. Lance was by no means perfect, but at least he worked hard and made an honest living. And he was rich.

Why dream of a worn-out green sofa? she wondered. Her leather sectional, and her new climate-controlled home, were much more comfortable. Luxurious. Brian represented a past of financial uncertainty, one she could not—and would never—go back to.

Schwartz's gruff voice recalled her to the present. "Happy holidays, young lady? Fuck that." He grabbed champagne flutes from a passing waiter for Lance, Cassidy, and himself. "Happy birthday, Jesus!"

Lance and Cassidy joined Schwartz in his profane toast. The Chicago Alderman downed the flute in one go, then looked at it suspiciously, as if he couldn't remember where the champagne had gone.

"There was something very important I was going to ask you," Schwartz muttered, his bleary eyes wandering upward in thought.

"About your congressional campaign?" prompted Lance. "I assure you, the campaign's financial channels are in place and the coffers are full. You can't lose."

"Lose?" repeated Schwartz. His mouth twisted in distaste, as if the word were wholly unfamiliar. "Son, I've never lost at anything in my life, much less an election. Besides, I've made a deal that will guarantee my victory." He double-tapped a finger on the side of his bulbous nose and winked. With his white beard and ponderous frame, he looked like a devilish Santa Claus.

"You're running for Congress?" asked Cassidy. "How exciting!"

"Indeed I am." Schwartz's eyes feasted on her, and he made no effort to hide it. "Washington needs fresh perspectives on immigration, national security, and criminal justice. We have to drain the swamp."

"I agree that the justice system needs an overhaul," said Cassidy. "What's your position on decriminalizing marijuana?"

Once again, Lance's face told her she'd said something out of line. Would this evening never end?

Schwartz snapped his fingers. "Now I remember what I was going to ask." He took Cassidy's right hand and pressed it too hard. "You, my dear, must come to the Bears game on Sunday. We'll watch the game from my luxury suite. And you too, Lance."

"Oh, Lance, could we?" asked Cassidy. Spending a day with the handsy Schwartz would be worth it to see the 9-4 Bears clinch the division with a victory. "The Bears are playing the Packers!"

"I hate to be a party-pooper," began Lance, "but Penelope and I leave for the airport on Monday for a deposition in New York. I have to be on my game."

Though crestfallen, Cassidy nodded. "I understand." She turned to Schwartz. "I'm afraid we can't make it."

Penelope Lambert was the firm's partnership committee chair, Lance's unofficial mentor, and someone who expected a close working relationship. Disappointing her, especially when Lance was on the cusp of making partner himself, would be a disaster for his career.

More importantly, Lance would be unfit to live with if the partnership vote didn't go his way. His foot might unexpectedly find Buster's ass, as it had one time before, after he'd lost an important case. Lance had sworn never, ever to do that again, but there was always the possibility of a second infraction.

"It's a noon game," said Schwartz. The man suddenly seemed quite sober, his voice edged. "You must come, Lance. And you have to bring your lovely bride. That's non-negotiable."

Cassidy could see the scowl beneath Lance's polite smile. He was between a rock and a hard place. Did he risk offending a client of Schwartz's caliber?

"Sure, we'll come."

"Excellent!" Schwartz seemed more relieved than excited. "Your wife's a good-luck charm, you understand. The last time she graced the presence of my suite, the Bears beat the Seahawks. Boy, what a game that was!"

Schwartz talked with them for a time before moving off in search of more booze. When he was gone, Lance took Cassidy by the elbow and pulled her behind the biggest Christmas tree she'd ever seen, out of earshot from his colleagues.

"Are you trying to fuck things up for me?" said Lance.

"What are you talking about?"

"To begin with, bringing up marijuana to Schwartz. He doesn't know you're the ex-wife of a guy who dealt drugs while in his employ, and he's never going to know that. No one here is ever going to know that. Got it?"

Cassidy didn't answer.

"Second, saying 'happy holidays' to Schwartz when he'd said, 'merry Christmas' first."

Cassidy crossed her arms. "You told me to say that, remember?"

"Don't tell me what I fucking said," whispered Lance. "You've got a brain in that pretty little head of yours, right? When an important client says it, you say it back."

Stress thought Cassidy. He's under tremendous stress. So many people are counting on him to perform, to win.

"I'm doing my best," she told him. "Can we go home?"

"Lastly, you never offer political opinions when you don't know the other person's position. What have I always said about asking questions?"

"Never ask a question you don't know the answer to," said Cassidy. "Are you being a complete asshole?"

"What?"

"See, I know the answer to that question." Her Irish eyes were sharper than chipped emeralds. "Here are some more: Who's sleeping on the sofa tonight? Who's about to get his face slapped before his wife storms out with the car keys?"

The Chameleon retreated from the field. He poured out an apology, claiming stress and lack of sleep had taken their toll. He didn't deserve her, she was an angel, they'd adopt a child one day, take a vacation, blah blah blah.

She caved, just as he knew she would.

"Well, well," called out a woman's voice, "whom do we have here, hiding like presents under a Christmas tree?"

The Chameleon changed again, immediately going into the character of cheerful subordinate. He smiled broadly at the speaker, a handsome woman in a low-cut red dress.

"Hello, Penelope," said Lance. "You remember my wife, Cassidy?"

"How could I forget?" Penelope Lambert shook Cassidy's hand, leaned in, and kissed the air next to both cheeks. "This tall drink of water is my husband, Carl. Say hello, Carl."

"Hello, Carl," said Carl. He bowed stiffly and did not offer to shake hands. To Cassidy, Carl looked as out of place at this soirée as she did.

Penelope Lambert was a vivacious, full-figured woman of about fifty, with a pixie-cut of blonde hair that would have looked better on a younger woman. She was quick-witted and talked very fast.

Lance kept up with his mentor, trading verbal ripostes that made Cassidy's head swim. She tried to join in, but often had no idea who or what they were talking about. Carl busied himself by keeping his wife's champagne flute filled. Between fetching her drinks, the man decimated half a cheese log all by himself.

"You'll have to forgive Carl," said Penelope. "He's the strong, silent type. I've been dragging him to these parties for years, and he's bored. Aren't you, Carl?"

She'd caught Carl sticking a cracker piled with caviar into his mouth. He gulped it down and said, "I'm not bored. It's that I don't have anything in common with most people here. They all want to talk cases or politics."

Penelope caught Cassidy's nod of agreement. "Let's change the subject, for the benefit of the non-attorneys. How did the two of you meet?"

Before Cassidy could respond, Lance jumped in. "Cassidy was walking her dog one day when he slipped his leash. Poor thing ran into a busy street and was this close to a one-way trip to doggy heaven. I ran into the street, grabbed Buster, and brought him back safe and sound."

Cassidy's jaw fell open in complete shock. Brian had rescued Buster on that terrible day. She doubted Lance would run into danger for Buster or for anyone else for that matter. Including herself. But she wisely closed her mouth while Lance embellished the stolen story.

"I guess there are heroes left in the world," said Penelope. She was smiling at Lance in a funny way.

"Carl," asked Lance, "what are your interests?"

"All Carl knows is engineering and football," answered Penelope.

Cassidy brightened. "You're a Bears fan, too? Lance and I are going to the game this Sunday."

"We're gonna beat the Pack's ass this time!" said Carl. "Playoffs, here we come."

Penelope clapped her hands in delight. "My dear, you've found a kindred spirit." She regarded Cassidy with a glazed look from too much drinking. "I need to borrow your husband for a few minutes to go over the finer points of Monday's deposition. There's a memo I need to fetch from my office. Will you entertain Carl while we're gone?"

Cassidy glanced to Lance. Her husband seemed nervous under a tight-lipped smile. He nodded to her.

"Of course."

"There's a dear," said Penelope. "I'll bring him back in one piece." She wrapped her arm around his elbow and the two of them disappeared into a hallway.

Their departure from the party had not gone unnoticed by other members of the firm. Cassidy saw people elbowing each other, whispering when they passed. Others nodded, as if privy to a secret she did not know. From across the room, Claude Schwartz eyed her above the rim of his drink, his look a mixture of pity and lust.

Carl pulled up two chairs and motioned for her to have a seat. Cassidy sat down, crossing her legs and trying to position her purse to cover herself. The little black dress Lance had picked was riding up her thighs, leaving her feeling exposed to the world.

Cassidy and Carl talked about the Bears' chances this year to make the Super Bowl. Cassidy thought New Orleans or Los Angeles might be the biggest stumbling blocks, while Carl mistrusted the sneaky-good Cowboys.

Less than ten minutes later, Penelope and Lance rejoined the party. Penelope looked flushed, while Lance appeared disheveled.

"If you need a good divorce lawyer," said Carl, "I have several I could recommend."

December 16, 2018, 11:46 a.m.
Soldier Field, Chicago

Brian Piccolo thrust his mop into the wringer and pulled down the mechanism's handle. The wringer squeezed, and a mixture of water and cleaning solution gushed into a bucket. He took out the mop and once again started cleaning the floor in front of a men's restroom. He'd cleaned the spot several times already this morning, and he'd probably clean it several times more before the day was done. It was funny to him that nobody noticed this strange behavior. Tommy was right: people wearing uniforms and doing dirty jobs were practically invisible to everyone else.

In front of the restroom, Brian had placed two bright yellow signs. The first read *Restroom Closed for Maintenance* and the second read *Caution: Wet Floor* in several languages.

Though kickoff was a few minutes away, this section of Soldier Field was practically deserted. Earlier in the day, before the crowds were let in, Brian had taken his janitorial cart (a jumbo-sized trashcan, mop and wheeled bucket, and various cleaning supplies) to the hallway servicing the luxury suites on the eastern side of the stadium. This men's restroom was the closest one to the suite used by Claude Schwartz.

Several men had already come by to use the restroom, only to find Brian busily mopping the entrance. One of them had tried to slip through, but Brian stepped in front of him.

"Believe me, you don't want to go in there." Brian pinched his own nose and waved a hand at an imaginary bad smell.

"I gotta take a leak," said the man. "Drain the main vein. I'll be careful."

"Not here, pal," said Brian. "Floor's wet. Look, it's my neck if you go in there and bust your ass. You go to the hospital, maybe lawyer up, and I go to the unemployment bureau. We don't want that, do we?"

The man was about to push by but blanched at the steely look on Brian's face. "I'll find another one."

"Have a great day," said Brian. "Go Bears!"

"Go Bears!" repeated the man as he walked away.

"That was close," said a muffled voice.

Brian didn't respond. There was no one around, save for himself. He went back to mopping. The sloshing sounds were occasionally interrupted by the disembodied voice of the stadium announcer over the public address system.

Brian scratched at his beard. In three months, it had grown thick as the wool on a black ram. With the glasses he wore, he doubted that his own mother would recognize him, God rest her soul.

Under his white jacket, the Beretta M9A3 rested snugly in a specially designed holster provided by Tommy. The gun was fitted with the suppressor and fully loaded, including a round in the chamber. That made eleven hollow point rounds to get the job done. He hoped he wouldn't need nearly that many.

"Hey, Brian," said the muffled voice. "Have they kicked off yet? I've got a hunny riding on the Bears."

"Rico!" said Brian. "Shut up before someone hears you."

"It's cramped in here."

In answer, Brian kicked the jumbo-sized trashcan, and the voice fell silent. Brian leaned against his mop and looked down the hallway at the doors leading to the suites. Behind the closest door, Claude Schwartz would soon be entertaining two very special guests.

Brian swallowed hard, wondering again if he'd have the nerve to shoot someone in cold blood.

Cold blood. That was a funny expression. In the movies, that's what they said about people who committed premeditated murder. Killers who lay in wait for their victims, knowing full well what they were doing to the last detail. But Brian's blood didn't run cold when he thought about the years taken from his life, served up by Lance Kincaid as the fall guy for the sins of

Claude Schwartz. He didn't feel cold when he pictured Cassidy in Lance's bed.

No. In such moments, Brian's blood boiled in rage, and his hands ached to kill Lance Kincaid. It was Kincaid who'd stolen Cassidy from him. Kincaid who was supposed to be Brian's advocate in the criminal justice system. Kincaid who'd advised him to take a plea and sign a bogus confession to protect Schwartz.

Tommy's organization had confirmed the connection between Kincaid and Schwartz. The Alderman was known to them as a major player in the drug trade, using his delivery vans to move product safely all over the city. As it turned out, they had tipped the cops to raid Brian's van in the hopes of taking down Schwartz and reducing the competition. Kincaid's duplicity had derailed that plan, enraging the underworld.

Since framing Schwartz had failed, Tommy convinced his superiors to cut the man a deal: in exchange for clearing the field of Schwartz's competitors in the congressional primaries, through bribery or other means, the alderman would get out of the drug trade. He'd also give them Lance Kincaid.

Speak of the devil.

Lance and Cassidy were walking toward Brian, not ten yards away. Lance had a sour look on his face as he stared at a phone, hardly watching where he was going. Cassidy was dressed in a vintage Bears jersey, sporting #34 for Sweetness, Walter Payton. She had a faraway look on her face that was as sad as it was distant.

Brian froze, wondering if they'd recognize him through the beard, glasses, and uniform. But they didn't give him a second glance, let alone a first one, as they entered Schwartz's suite and shut the door.

December 16, 2018, 11:55 a.m.
Soldier Field, Chicago

"I'm so pleased you've come," said Schwartz as Lance and Cassidy Kincaid entered his suite. "Make yourselves at home. I've taken the liberty of ordering some refreshments."

An assortment of bottled beers, dripping with condensation, protruded from ice buckets. There was a steaming deep-dish pizza, giant salted pretzels, and mustards for dipping.

The view from the suite was as spectacular as Cassidy remembered. The crowd seemed to be a living organism of dark navy and orange, the Bears' team colors, with pockets of green and gold for the Packers. The air was electric, filling her with excitement.

On the field, the team captains for the Bears and Packers were assembled for the coin toss. The referee's voice came over the intercom as he asked the visiting team to make the call.

"Thanks for inviting us, Claude," said Lance. The sour look had been replaced with a small smile. Cassidy recognized it for what it was, the fake grin Lance seemed to keep in his back pocket to mask his true feelings.

Today, he was feeling...what? Annoyance?

It was hard to tell. He'd been moody ever since the Holiday Mixer and his impromptu meeting with Penelope Lambert. Instead of the usual emotional cocktail of stress and irritation, he seemed subdued. Emasculated. Nothing Cassidy did could cheer him up, even serving him his favorite breakfast in bed, followed by riotous sex. This was a tiresome Lance Kincaid.

Cassidy was still unsure what she'd seen between her husband and his mentor. Had that been harmless flirtation? Or something more? The whispers and stares of Lance's fellow attorneys seemed to say it was something salacious. Scandalous, even. She also remembered the lustful look of Claude Schwartz. It reminded her of the hunger on Penelope's face when she led Lance away.

"Sit next to me, Cassidy," said Schwartz. "You're my good-luck charm today, remember?"

"Thank you, Mr. Schwartz." She took a seat next to their host. Lance flopped down beside her, looking bored.

"Call me Claude."

"Sure. Claude."

On the field, Green Bay won the coin toss and elected to defer. Good. The Bears would get the ball first.

"Who else is coming?" asked Lance. "Last time, you were packing them in like sardines."

"You're the first to arrive," said Schwartz. "I hear there's a traffic snarl on the expressway. Might be only us for the time being."

Lance frowned at this but said nothing. He stood up abruptly. "Where's the restroom?"

"The nearest is right outside the door, to the left. You can't miss it."

"Thanks. Save me some pizza, will you?"

Lance closed the door behind him. On the field, the Bears had first-and-ten at the Green Bay 47. Cassidy tried to focus on the game instead of Schwartz's uncomfortable proximity.

Schwartz popped open two Fat Tires, setting one next to her. "I remember you liked amber ales and salted pretzels. Am I right?"

"Yes, on both counts." She took the bottle and brought it to her lips for a long swig. Its refreshing flavor calmed her nerves.

"Try the honey mustard on a pretzel," said Schwartz. He followed his own advice by taking a pretzel and dipping it into a jar. His pale blue eyes were charming, almost playful.

Cassidy took a pretzel, dipped it in honey mustard, and took a bite. It melted in her mouth. This, she thought as she looked around the suite, was living the high life.

"Sweetness," said Schwartz. "A fitting choice for such a sweet woman."

"What?"

"Your jersey."

"Oh," said Cassidy. "He's my favorite Bear."

"My wife loved watching Payton run." Schwartz absently twisted the wedding band on his hand. "So smooth. She laughed her ass off when The Fridge tried to carry Payton over the goal line for a touchdown. You remember the play?"

Cassidy laughed. "That was a riot. I didn't know you were married, Claude."

"Bernadette died ten years ago. Breast cancer."

"I'm sorry. I lost my mother to cancer last summer." Cassidy reached over and patted Schwartz's hand. It was weathered and rough, covered with hair. But it was not an unpleasant hand.

On the field, the Bears' offence had stalled on the Green Bay 48. The punt went forty-four yards to the Green Bay 4, pinning the Packers deep in their own territory.

Cassidy did not jump up and pump her fists, as she might have done had she been watching the game at home. Instead, her hand remained on Claude's, gently squeezing it.

Brian was wringing out his mop for the umpteenth time when he spotted Kincaid exiting the suite. He and Cassidy had gone in a few minutes earlier, but Brian had not gotten a good look at them. The attorney was dressed in a Bears hoodie, jeans, and white Nike tennis shoes. Exactly as Tommy's spotter had texted. Perfect.

Kincaid began walking toward him. Brian quickly picked up the two yellow signs—the ones reading *Restroom Closed for Maintenance* and *Caution: Wet Floor*—and set them on his janitorial cart.

"Is the restroom open?" asked Kincaid.

"Yes, sir," said Brian, turning his back and pretending to rearrange items on his cart. "All finished up, spick and span. Go right in."

Brian turned around, but the man wasn't there. He'd walked in somewhere between "yes" and "sir." With a grunt, Brian wheeled the cart into the restroom, picked up the two signs, and placed them on the floor outside. Blocking the entrance.

Kincaid was standing in front of a urinal, pants unzipped, studying the wall. The restroom was deserted except for them, as it had been all morning, thanks to Brian's signs. It was quiet, except for the monitors perched in the corners that were broadcasting the game. Occasionally, the roar of the crowd pounded in like an ocean wave.

Brian knocked on the jumbo-sized trashcan on his cart.

"Get out, Rico," he whispered.

A tall man stood up in the trashcan, disturbing the mountain of wadded paper towels that had covered him. Rico stiffly lifted first one leg and then the other out of the can, groaning. He was wearing the same style hoodie as Kincaid, with jeans and white tennis shoes.

Brian looked Rico up and down, smiling. "Dead ringer."

"That was brutal," said Rico in a low voice, stretching his arms. "This had better be worth it."

"You're getting the keys to a 2018 Mercedes-Benz AMG SUV, worth a quarter of a million dollars," answered Brian. "So, stop complaining."

Kincaid had flushed the urinal and was washing his hands. Slowly, he turned his head to Brian and Rico. He raised up, not shutting off the water.

"If you two queers are looking for action," said Kincaid, "move along."

"This guy's an asshole," said Rico. "I can see why you want to kill him."

"Hello, Lance," said Brian. He unholstered the Beretta from under his jacket, flipped the safety, and pointed it at Kincaid. "Check the hallway, Rico. Whistle if you see anyone."

"You got it, Brian."

"Brian?" said Kincaid. "Brian fucking Piccolo?"

Brian groaned. His slow reveal had just been ruined by Rico, the simple-minded idiot. The big speech he'd dreamed about, rehearsed ad nauseam, out the window. Oh well. He'd have to settle for killing Lance Kincaid without a dramatic speech.

Kincaid wore a smirk on his face rather than fear.

"The beard's a nice touch, Brian. Holy shit, it's good to see you."

The muzzle of the Beretta dropped imperceptibly. This wasn't the reaction Brian was expecting. He'd had visions of Kincaid begging for his life, groveling.

"I did my best for you, Brian," said Kincaid. He was facing Brian now, fifteen feet away, standing on the balls of his feet. "I hope you know that. Put the gun down, my friend, and let's talk it out."

"Pop him, Brian," called out Rico. "Every second you're standing here is a second too long."

"Don't listen to your handsome friend," said Kincaid. "You're a good guy, I knew that the moment we met. A decent, upstanding citizen. You're not a killer."

"He's playing you," said Rico.

Kincaid took a step forward, palms up, eyes on the gun. It was beginning to shake in Brian's hand.

"Schwartz is the one you want, not me," said Kincaid. "He's here today, you know. Sitting in that sweet luxury box. Your boss had me by the balls, Brian. I didn't want to sell you up the river, but I had no other choice. We're both victims here."

"Bullshit," said Brian. "You fucked me over. Then you stole Cassidy from me."

Brian cocked the gun.

The clicking sound sent a shudder through Kincaid, and for the first time he seemed unsure of himself. Then he reattached his smile as if it were a mask.

"Your wife was in dire financial straits," said Kincaid as he began edging forward again, "with a mortgage she couldn't afford and a sick mother. Would you want her on the streets, waiting three years? That's pretty selfish, don't you think?"

Kincaid kept talking. Brian felt the sweat between his hand and the gun. It felt like it weighed a thousand pounds.

He knew he should pull the trigger. But Kincaid's words were swirling around his head, confusing him. Had Schwartz forced Kincaid's hand? Was it fair to let Cassidy suffer alone? The attorney sounded so logical, so reasonable.

Disarming.

Kincaid lunged for him, mid-sentence, his head down and arms forward. Brian stepped back, dropped the muzzle of the gun to Kincaid's torso, and fired twice.

Kincaid's momentum kept him falling forward. Brian stepped out of his path, letting the body roll to the floor, the head smacking the tile. Cautiously, Brian rolled the body over with his foot. The attorney's eyes stared vacantly at the ceiling, legs twitching.

Rico walked over. "Deader than a doornail," he said. He fished a wallet, phone, and keys out of the dead man's pockets. "Hey, nice watch. Gold-plated Swiss Jaeger-LeCoultre. And it fits perfectly."

"Help me get him into the trashcan," said Brian. He'd already retrieved the two casings ejected by the gun. Brian and Rico hefted the body up, and Kincaid slid silently into the can.

Brian grabbed his mop. There was very little blood on the floor. Kincaid's back had been clear, so the hollow points had not exited the body.

"Get going, Rico," said Brian. "Don't talk to anyone, walk to the exit, and drive away in Kincaid's car. It's yours."

"I'll wave to the security cameras as I go," said Rico.

"You'll do no such thing," said Brian. "The cameras are going to see Lance Kincaid walking out of here, not some goofy bastard waving to them. Understand?"

"Got it. Nice doing business with you."

Brian stuck his mop into the wringer and pulled the handle. The crowd roared, and he looked to a monitor for the replay. Green Bay's quarterback Aaron Rodgers was on his back with the football, sacked by Chicago's Kahlil Mack.

Brian broke into the Super Bowl Shuffle.

Episode 6½
Subscriber Exclusive

PLATANOS CON LECHERA AND A SNUB-NOSED .38

Michael Bracken

Carmine Monteleone dialed a number he had memorized two decades earlier, and a voice he didn't recognize answered. He asked, "What's the word on Bobby Bananas?"

"Bobby Bananas?" asked the voice on the other end of the line. "Who the hell is Bobby Bananas?"

"Talk to Don Giodano, he'll tell you," Carmine said. "I'll call back tomorrow. You tell me if the contract is still open."

"Giancarlo's dead."

"Fuck. Who took him out?"

"Cancer," said the voice on the other end. "Right in the gut."

"Who replaced him?"

"Who the hell are you to be asking all these questions?"

"I worked for the Don."

"Then how come you don't know he's dead?"

Carmine didn't want to admit his physical and mental deterioration to some yutz whose voice he didn't recognize. "I been away for a few years. That's all you need to know. I'll call back tomorrow. Same time."

He disconnected the call before the other man could question him again, and he sat staring at the phone until a nurse's aide tapped him on the shoulder, startling him so badly he almost shit in his diaper.

Carmine spun around. "What the fuck do you want?"

A skinny blonde younger than his replacement hip smiled and said, "Lunch time, Mr. Monteleone. Your favorite."

His favorite was strawberry Ensure and Jack Daniels, but he pretended to like the spaghetti and meatballs with the watery sauce the home served every Wednesday. He turned and followed the little blonde to the dining room.

Late that afternoon, Carmine's son Eddie found him sitting on a bench in the garden behind the nursing home. He took one whiff of his father, settled on the bench upwind of the old man, and said, "I got a problem."

"You got a problem? I'm sitting in my own shit and my only son doesn't even say hello before he starts bitching about something."

"The money's gone. They're going to kick you out at the end of the month."

"I got a worse problem."

"Worse than being kicked out?"

"I saw Bobby Bananas yesterday."

"Well, I saw Andy Apple and Betty Blackberry in the foyer," Eddie said. "You could get 'em together and make a fruit salad."

"You think I'm being funny?"

"You ain't ever been funny."

"I need you to get me a gun."

"What're you going to do, stage a breakout?" Eddie asked. "They're kicking you out at the end of the month, and you sure as hell can't live with us. We tried that before. Michelle would take the girls and leave if I even suggested it."

"Would you shut up and pay attention," Carmine said. "I need you to get me a gun so I can take care of Bobby Bananas before someone else does."

"You going to shoot a man lives here?" Eddie looked around. "He's probably half dead already."

"Half dead ain't all dead," Carmine said, "and I need to make him all dead."

Eddie said nothing.

"Well?"

"I can't even make next week's car payment. Where am I going to get the money for a gun?"

"You do this for me and it's the last thing I'll ever ask from you," Carmine said. "It's the last thing I'll ever need to ask from you."

At a quarter to midnight, Eddie Monteleone stood at the window of a taco truck parked in Cicero, a long way from his home in Itasca. He had a wad of small bills in his pocket, much of it taken without their knowledge from his daughters' piggy banks.

The pasty-faced guy staring at him from inside the taco truck looked like he'd been repeatedly hit in the face with the flat side of a shovel, and Eddie felt certain he could count all of the guy's teeth without ever reaching double digits. From the guy's mush mouth came, "Yeah?"

Eddie glanced at the menu. "The special. The dessert special."

"*Platanos con lechera?*"

"Yeah, sure." Eddie dug the wad of bills from his pocket and placed it on the counter. "I want the *special* special."

Mush mouth narrowed his eyes. "Do we know you?"

"You Jesse?" Eddie asked. When Mush mouth nodded, he continued, "My father said you'd know him. Carmine Monteleone."

"You're Carmine's boy?

Eddie shifted nervously. He'd never had anything to do with his father's business, and when he'd grown old enough to know what his father did, he'd wanted nothing to do with it. He nodded.

"We all thought Carmine was dead." Mush mouth shouted over his shoulder to the anemic blonde working the grill. "It's Carmine's boy."

The blonde leaned back so she could look out the window at Eddie. "Looks just like him when he was younger. That Carmine could set a young girl's heart on fire. And her crotch, too. The son-of-a-bitch gave me the clap. What's he want?"

"The dessert special."

"I'm on it." She dropped a dollop of butter on the grill. Then she sliced a pair of bananas in half, dropped them on the sizzling butter, and covered them with cinnamon.

Mush mouth look at something under the counter and then asked. "A close-up job?"

Eddie shrugged.

"Must be," Mush mouth said as he scooped the cash off the counter. "Your daddy always liked to work close-up."

A moment later he placed a white take-out bag on the counter and next to it placed a plastic dish filled with cinnamon fried bananas covered with sweetened condensed milk. Eddie collected both, grabbed a plastic fork, and ate the *platanos con lechera* before driving away.

Carmine glanced around before he lifted the phone and dialed the same number as he had the day before. Before the yutz on the other end could say anything, Carmine said, "Bobby Bananas."

"A hundred Gs," said the yutz. "Baby Don Giodano said the contract's so old—"

"Baby Don?"

"Took over for his father."

"Here's how it's going down," Carmine said.

He explained how he expected delivery of payment after he completed the contract. Then he disconnected the call and shuffled to the dining room for meatloaf, mashed potatoes, and a conversation with Mrs. Williams, whose son worked as an undercover detective and visited her every Saturday afternoon.

That afternoon, in Carmine's private room, Eddie handed the take-out bag to his father.

Carmine opened the bag and looked at the snub-nosed .38 inside. Then he looked at his son. "You didn't touch it did you?"

"Fuck no."

"And if anybody ever asks, you don't know nothing about it." Carmine lifted out the revolver and handed the empty bag to his son. "You take this out of here and burn it."

Eddie wadded up the bag and shoved it in his pocket. "What'd this Bananas guy do?"

"Ratted out Antonio Giodano and disappeared into WitSec. Old Man Giodano died in prison. The family vowed vengeance, but nobody could ever get a line on Bobby Bananas until now."

"And you think he's here?"

"I know he's here."

Eddie shook his head. "I'll see you next Wednesday. We'll talk about what we're going to do at the end of the month when we can't pay for next month."

"You don't worry about that," Carmine said. "I got it all worked out."

Carmine waited until Saturday afternoon, when a warm breeze came off the lake and many of the home's residents were in the garden behind the home. He slipped the .38 into the pocket of his robe, downed a strawberry Ensure and Jack Daniel's cocktail, and then shuffled outside.

Twenty minutes later he found Bobby Bananas sitting in a wheelchair watching a pair of aides struggling to help one of the other residents to her feet after a fall. He approached the wheelchair-bound man from behind.

"That you, Carmine?" Bobby asked without looking back. "I can smell you coming."

"Well, I could smell a rat the first time I saw you in the dining room," he glanced around and saw Mrs. Weaver visiting with her son. "I almost lost my appetite."

"Well, fuck you, too."

Carmine pulled the snub-nosed .38 from his robe pocket and pressed the barrel against the base of the other man's skull.

"Do it," Bobby said. "You'll be doing me a favor."

"Be doing both of us a favor," Carmine said. "You got any last words?"

"Fuck you and the walker you hobbled in on."

Carmine squeezed the trigger twice, spreading Bobby Bananas' brains across the lawn.

Staff, residents, and visitors scrambled for cover. Mrs. Weaver's son, the undercover detective, ran against the tide of people, drawing his sidearm as he approached Carmine.

"Put the gun down, old man!"

"Fuck you, copper!"

Carmine jerked the .38 upward, but his finger wasn't on the trigger. Mrs. Weaver's son reacted, squeezing off a single shot that dropped Carmine to his knees. He fell forward, onto his face, and died having successfully completed his last job.

Chicago police did not immediately identify the dead man in the wheelchair as Bobby "Bananas" Columbo, but a detective pushing retirement learned of the faded Miss Chiquita tattoo on the dead man's left bicep, and research into several cold cases confirmed the identity of the man whose testimony had led to Antonio Giodano's lifelong prison sentence.

Detectives repeatedly interviewed Carmine's son but were unable to indict Eddie as an accessory to Bobby Bananas' murder. Rather than waste precious manpower on an open-and-shut case that ended in the deaths of two aging mid-level mafiosos, they wrote it up as a murder followed by a suicide-by-cop and closed the case.

By the time the police stopped harassing Eddie and his family, he had lost his car and was daily fending off calls from bill collectors. After his wife learned that Eddie had drained their daughters' piggy banks and he refused to tell her what he had done with the money, she threatened to take the girls with her to her parents' home in Indianapolis.

Eddie had remained on the right side of the law his entire life, but nothing he did seemed to be working out. So, he was considering returning to the taco truck, purchasing a piece, and sticking up a couple of convenience stores.

Then one evening he answered a knock and opened his front door to find himself facing two men in dark suits. The shorter one held a gym bag. The taller one asked, "You Carmine Monteleone's son?"

"Yeah."

The shorter one shoved the gym bag into his arms. "This is yours."

As they turned to leave, Eddie asked, "What is this?"

"Your father's last paycheck."

Eddie closed the door, opened the gym bag, and found one hundred thousand dollars in small bills. He turned and shouted, "Honey, I think my father just solved our problems."

BOOKS

On the following pages are a few
more great titles from the
Down & Out Books publishing family.

For a complete list of books and to
sign up for our newsletter,
go to DownAndOutBooks.com.

The Stone Carrier
Robert Ward

Down & Out Books
January 2020
978-1-64396-052-4

A wild, funny and terrifying nonstop thriller set in the wild days of the 1970s when New York was adrift in snow, sex and violence.

Terry Brennan is usually the one writing about the scene but now he IS the scene, a reporter who is suddenly the subject of a murder investigation. His best friend from childhood Ray Gardello is dead, and he is the prime suspect. He's on the run and both the cops and Nicky Baines, Harlem's most violent drug dealer is closing in.

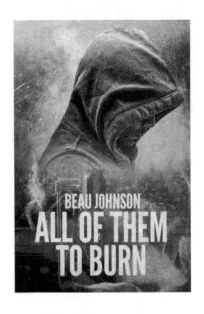

All of Them to Burn
Beau Johnson

Down & Out Books
February 2020
978-1-64396-091-3

Darkness is an attribute most of us rally against. It can consume. It can achieve. But if we so choose, it can also be held at bay.

Enter Bishop Rider and the evil he's chosen to obliterate since his family is taken from him. Operating outside the law, circumventing a system beyond repair, Bishop stalks this darkness the only way he knows how. Not only because these men deserve what he's become, but because of a message he attempted to create has come back to haunt him, now, after all these years. It's this story, along with other, unconnected tales that populate _All of Them to Burn_.

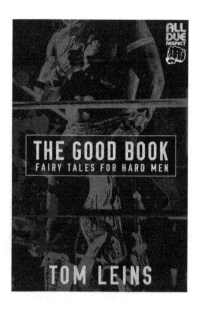

The Good Book
Fairy Tales for Hard Men
Tom Leins

All Due Respect, an imprint of
Down & Out Books
January 2020
978-1-64396-054-8

The Good Book is an interlinked, 20-story collection that takes place between 1980 and 1993 and focuses on the stars of the Testament Wrestling Alliance.

These stories are grubby, hardboiled tales that explore the lives of desperate men—men who can't leave their rivalries in the ring. In Testament, every action has a reaction, every feud ends in carnage and the road to hell is paved with dead wrestlers.

Chasing China White
Allan Leverone

Shotgun Honey, an imprint of
Down & Out Books
September 2019
978-1-64396-029-6

When heroin junkie Derek Weaver runs up an insurmountable debt with his dealer, he's forced to commit a home invasion to wipe the slate clean.

Things go sideways and Derek soon finds himself a multiple murderer in the middle of a hostage situation.

With seemingly no way out, he may discover the key to redemption lies in facing down long-ignored demons.

CPSIA information can be obtained
at www.ICGtesting.com
Printed in the USA
FSHW011818140220
67017FS

9 781643 961262